Sensible
Physics
Teaching

Sensible
Physics
Teaching

Michael D'Aleo
Stephen Edelglass

Illustrations by Matthew Lanci

A Science and Mathematics Association
for Research and Teaching Book

Waldorf
PUBLICATIONS
RESEARCH INSTITUTE FOR WALDORF EDUCATION

Printed with support from the Waldorf Curriculum Fund

Published by:
Waldorf Publications at the
Research Institute for Waldorf Education
38 Main Street
Chatham, NY 12037

Title: *Sensible Physics Teaching*
   A Science and Mathematics Association
   for Research and Teaching Book
Authors: Michael D'Aleo and Stephen Edelglass
Illustrations: Matthew Lanci
Layout: Ann Erwin
Proofreading: Ruth Riegel

Acknowledgements

We are extremely indebted to Manfred von Mackensen who, with great generosity, allowed us to use whatever material we wished from his three-volume series, *A Phenomena-Based Physics*. We made liberal use of this offer, which we very much appreciated.

We wish to thank the Cultural Freedom Foundation, the Science and Mathematics Association for Research and Teaching and the Saratoga Experiential Natural Science Research Institute for generous support, financial and otherwise. They not only made this book possible but also encouraged us to present the conference/workshop *Teaching Sensible Physics* in July 1998. The many excellent questions and comments by the teachers who attended that conference significantly helped to make this book easier to use. We thank them.

We especially appreciate Matthew Lanci's illustrations. He made most of the drawings in the summer following his completion of the eighth grade at the Spring Hill Waldorf School in Saratoga Springs, NY. His enthusiasm for this project was boundless.

We also thank Hanna Edelglass for her unstinting work editing the Introduction to make it clearer and more precise in countless ways.

MICHAEL D'ALEO
STEPHEN EDELGLASS

We dedicate this book to our wives:
Sigrid and Hanna

Contents

    Sound – Acoustics
    Visual Experience – Optics
    Warmth and Cold
    Electricity and Magnetism

    Warmth and Cold
    Visual Experience – Optics
    Electrical Phenomena
    Mechanics

    Warmth – Thermal Physics
    Visual Phenomena – Refraction
    Hydraulics and Aero-Mechanics
    Electromagnetism

Preface to the 2017 Edition

This book is kindly being reprinted by Waldorf Publications almost 20 years after its original inception. This printing retains all of the original language and experiments as well as the illustrations. The book has acted as a guidebook for the middle school science training, Teaching Sensible Science. This course and book have been found to be very valuable to the teacher participants as they prepare to teach the middle grades sciences. Further information about these courses can be found on the SENSRI website at www.sensri.org. Attention is also drawn to the Science Kits available from Waldorf Publications. These kits provide teachers and schools with most of the materials mentioned in this book and can be purchased as complete kits for each grade.

While the book continues to help teachers over all these years, life brings many changes to each of us in time. Stephen Edelglass passed away in 2000, a few years after the publication of this book. It is with great gratitude that I recall Stephen's colleagueship and efforts to produce this book, and I hope that this new printing is helpful to the many teachers who continually strive to bring the sciences to life in Waldorf schools.

– Michael D'Aleo
January 2017

Introduction to Sense-Based Science

The sun rose early on the lake at the beginning of the summer. A man and a woman loaded their packs of food, clothing and equipment into the canoe. The lake was smooth that morning. It looked well polished. The air was very still and fresh smelling. All was quiet except for the occasional call of an early morning bird. With a final soft thud the last pack was loaded into the canoe. The scraping of its bottom on the coarse sandy beach echoed across the lake as the canoe was launched. Immediately the sound was swallowed by the stillness.

In front of them the two trees along the shore were perfectly reflected, while those mirrored behind swayed in the soft wake. Most trees were pines, standing tall and straight as children do when you measure their height. A tree had fallen, a casualty of a strong storm that had long since passed. Its trunk pointed downward along the inclined bank. Where it entered the water the trunk appeared to be angled upward as if the submerged part were reaching for the surface like a fish looking for flies.

The woman in the stern noticed that, like the fallen tree, the paddles appeared to be bent and reaching for the surface. Although the paddles were made of strong, tough hickory, she observed them bend forward toward the surface when first plunged into the water and bend backward toward the surface at the end of the stroke. The bending was affected by the angle the paddle made with the surface: the more horizontal the paddle, the greater the bending.

With a loud splash a large bird dove into the lake. When it emerged from the water it flew to the far shore with something in its talons. Both boaters stopped paddling and raised their binoculars. Through the lenses they could make out the smooth, shiny body of the trout that the osprey had just caught.

As they observed the bird the canoe drifted toward the shore where the water was shallow. Many large fish were visible, while small fish were occasionally seen darting between the rocks, alerted by the canoe's shadow and looking for cover from the boat overhead. The water looked so shallow that it seemed certain the canoe would scrape on the rocks. Against their expectations, it did not. By pushing their paddles against the rocks, the canoeists slowly moved out into deeper water. Trying a final thrust, however, the two found that the paddles went deep into the water but did not reach the rock. The paddlers almost lost their balance when they did not meet the expected resistance. Having recovered, and now being in deeper water, they again paddled steadily. Looking down they noticed something else. At the middle of a stroke, when perpendicular to the water's surface, the paddles looked straight but seemed *shorter*.

The canoe settled into its smooth gliding rhythm, the paddler in the bow observing the world reflected in the lake, and the paddler in the stern contemplating the unusual pliable characteristics of the image of a paddle viewed below the surface as it moved through the water.

Sense-Based Science

Sense-based science originates, as do most scientific disciplines, with the experience of phenomena. Ideally, such experience is gained by way of an awakened state in which each human sense is active in gaining a perception. Understanding consists of joining concepts with sensing to gain perceptions of the world.

A phenomenon is a single experience or event of which human beings can be aware with their senses. It might be a sound or a color. A phenomenon might be the result of a complex sense experience, involving color, form, movement, sound, smell, surface texture, etc., such as the phenomenon of a deer in the woods. Awareness of a phenomenon depends upon the physical capacity of human beings to sense and, upon their intention, to pay attention to something extracted out of the phenomenal totality. Awareness of sense experience also depends on bringing conceptual relations to bear so that the sense world is organized into understandable experience. In other words, a concept is needed to actually see *some* thing as a *particular* thing. Imagine, for example, walking in the woods. A companion stops suddenly and whispers, "Look, a deer." Another responds, "Oh, I see it. It is hidden behind those trees in the brush." The baby in the pack on her father's back is, however, unable to see the deer no matter how patiently the others persist in pointing it out. Another companion may also not be able to see the deer because she is nearsighted.

In order to pick out the deer from the underbrush, the viewer must not only have the intention to look, but also know—i.e., have the concept of—what is looked for. That which is conjured in the mind, signified by the word *deer*, is the organizing idea that allows us to actually see the deer from out of the totality of impressions with which we are faced. It is this lack of its concept that prevents the baby from seeing the deer. Someone who never saw a deer might also just conceivably not be able to see the deer. However, the situation would quickly be remedied via the concepts of animal, feet, four, brown, tail, hoof, etc. In ordinary life we are usually unaware of the necessity of knowing what we are looking for before we are able to actually see it. Instead we see habitually, unconsciously taking for granted the context of a lifetime of experience gained from the time we ourselves were babies.

Although the emphasis in our examples has been predominantly visual, the concept "deer" includes important nonvisual sensible aspects, especially, but not only, those related to touch and warmth. For example, when we see a deer there is a feeling for the soft velvetness of a growing antler's sheath, so unlike the hard and smooth horn of a goat or cow. At the same time, because of unfamiliarity with the bellow of many types of deer, people often mistakenly take the sound the deer makes to be the bark of a dog. This is an instance of an inappropriate concept leading to an untrue perception.

Conscious experience of the sense world calls for being aware of the manifoldness of human sense capabilities, becoming conscious of the subtleties of each sense, and developing the intention to sense to the fullest, while being mindful of how intentions affect what we experience. The development of concepts that organize that experience and bring forth perceptions calls for flexibility and rigor of thought. Such concepts foster richer experience of the world as well as its understanding. Building the foundations for these capacities is the goal of sense-based science pedagogy in grades six, seven and eight.

Materials feel warmer to the touch after being exposed to bodies hotter than they are themselves. This is actually what warming (or heating) means. Similarly, material bodies feel colder to the touch when exposed to colder bodies. Materials also expand when pulled and contract when squeezed. Moreover, it is usually the case that when materials are warmed they also expand and when cooled they contract. (The behavior of water near its freezing point and of the metal bismuth, are exceptions to the principle that materials expand when they get hotter.) Nevertheless, temperature changes can occur without dimensional ones and vice versa. Becoming hotter/colder and expanding/contracting are really distinct experiences. (The great German thinker, Goethe, called such distinct experiences *archetypal phenomena*.) Still, a basis of temperature measurement is gained by associating qualitatively distinct experiences—expansion and contraction of the mercury column in a thermometer—with hotness and coldness.

Sense-based scientific methodology differs from much of the science taught today in that it steadfastly does not look behind the world of experience for an explanation. Most explanations today are in terms of mechanical models. For example, within a sense-based methodology the reason materials get hotter is understood to be that they are exposed to hotter bodies than they are themselves. This explanation consists of a description of the conditions under which to expect an experience. In contrast, an increase in hotness of a body is usually "explained" in terms of hypothetically faster-moving molecules of the hotter body colliding with the hypothetically slower-moving molecules of the colder body to increase the mean speed of the latter and decrease the mean speed of the former. Moreover, since the mean path of motion of faster-moving molecules is imagined to be larger than that of slower-moving ones, it follows that the expansion of material bodies accompanies their getting hotter. By using such hypothetical models, scientists feel they have "explained" the conjunction of increase of hotness and expansion.

However, model-based explanations are made at the expense of reducing hotness and coldness to the motion of hypothetical mechanical entities. In this way, hotness and coldness as such are implied to be merely subjective human responses. Molecules are taken to be real while human experience is not.

Molecules are not imagined to be either hot or cold. They are imagined just to move and collide with each other. Actually, molecules are merely *models* (imaginations) that constitute an intermediate virtual concept that is constructed mentally in order to "explain," among many other phenomena, why materials expand when they get hot. An intermediate nonperceptible entity (molecule) is created mentally to link a theorized cause-and-effect condition. The price of such an approach, however, is the alienation of human beings from the world of experience. In contrast, sense-based science places people directly into their experience. After all, experience is the final arbiter of the validity of scientific concepts.

In no way do the authors intend to convey the idea that models are useless. In fact, scientific models can be rather helpful. Much of our modern technology was developed using them. The objection we have to them is that when these intermediate virtual concepts are taken to constitute reality, a meaningful human context is lacking. This lack is, perhaps, one of the reasons that technology has not been an unalloyed blessing to the earth.

Consider the example of strong herbicides. While the chemical has the desired initial effect of killing unwanted plant life, such as weeds in lawns, the scientific community has been slow to react to its effect on wildlife and groundwater drinking supplies. There are, of course, many reasons for this, including the economic benefit to the producer and the convenience of chemicals to the user. However, we would suggest that one reason for the slowness of response is that because science is done in a manner that is abstracted from the experience of nature, human beings are simply less awake to the manifold character of that experience; they are less awake to its wholeness. By way of its emphasis on experience, the practice of sense-based science strengthens people's sense faculties. Thus, people are in the world actually rather than virtually.

The sense-based approach to science, via its emphasis on experience, naturally builds a relationship between the human being and the world. By requiring deeply engaged experience in its practice, sense-based science calls upon individuals to be more conscious of their own processes of perception. Developing the ability to experience phenomena richly, with greater consciousness, supports an increased ability to develop concepts that link the phenomena to each other. Such linking concepts are scientific laws. The process involves an active interweaving between the individual and the world. It results in a more thorough understanding of the relation between the world of subject and the world of object. Such scientific understanding is not biased by unconsciously assumed conditions placed on human knowledge that result in the alienation of human beings from the world in which we live.

The more usual method of science also has its beginnings in experience, but customary practice quickly moves toward imagining models of a world thought to exist "behind" the perceivable world. This imagined world is presumed to give rise to what is actually perceived. The validity of such a modeled world is determined by testing it in controlled experiments. When, according to the models, what is predicted to occur in a given set of circumstances actually does take place in the controlled experiment, scientists conclude that the model is correct and the phenomenon understood. The question "Why does that happen?" is answered in terms of behavior of the model.

The situation is analogous to that of experiencing the phenomenon of watch hands going round every minute and every hour and asking why that happens. We can imagine a number of clock mechanisms that might produce such behavior. However, we can only know what the mechanism actually is if we open the back of the watch, examine it and compare it to the imagined mechanism (model). We really only know the cause of the motion when the mechanism is actually perceived but such a perceived mechanism is of the phenomenal world, not behind it as are the imagined models of the world.

It is impossible to look behind the phenomenal world. Expecting scientific understanding to be of the form of an underlying model that explains experience presupposes that the world is like a machine that can be taken apart. Such a methodology encourages an *a priori* mechanical view of the world, a mechanical view that is supposed to make sense of life. What is more, such practice encourages concern with a virtual world of models rather than with the world of actual experience. Practice of such science removes human beings from their experience. It alienates them from reality.

Sense-based science, in contrast, encourages concern with actual experience and finding relationships within that experience. It encourages connectedness with other human beings and with the environment rather than detachment, because it stays within experience of human beings and their environment rather than looking behind such encounterings. Participation in the environment—human, natural and human-made—gives an immediate intuition for possible harmful effects of human action and, through that, self-knowledge.

The Pedagogical Significance of Sense-Based Science

Incredible growth and development characterize the first seven years of a child's life. During this time, children grow to at least five times their original height. They develop the ability to master their bodily movements. Children learn to move in their surroundings, unconsciously coordinating their sense of balance and visual images with the physical objects in the world. They also learn to speak and to listen, gaining a sophisticated, if unconscious, understanding of spoken language while imitating the people they hear in the environment.

During the elementary school years children develop strong imaginative faculties. With the beginning of formal schooling a new learning style emerges. Children acquire knowledge inspired by the love, trust and respect they have for the adults in their lives. Children can begin to feel that the world is inherently ordered and beautiful. During the first elementary grades children learn basic cultural elements: the alphabet, reading, writing and arithmetic, and myths, legends and stories pertaining to the culture in which they, and others, live.

However, as children approach age twelve they are less whole-heartedly inspired by the examples of the adults they know. Teachers and parents who have been involved with sixth grade students know the children are well aware that the beloved adults in their lives don't know everything. In fact, at times adults are wrong!

At that age, questioning and criticism can only occur when the student's faculties for perceiving phenomena become fittingly acute for critical thought to emerge. Sixth graders still hold on to the wonder of the world that characterized their earlier years. But, from the sixth into the ninth grades, wonder is replaced by critical thought and focused awareness. It is only when the student begins to take hold of these latter powers that he or she begins to ask questions such as "How do you know this is true?" Inwardly, they seek to know "Whom can I trust? Is the world as the adults say it is? If so, how is it that they are sometimes wrong?"

A child's inward seeking starts unconsciously through sense experiences that gain them percepts, almost as a feeling. But as children progress into adolescence, the inquiry becomes more conceptualized so that, by the time they are ninth graders, students are often able to verbalize these questions. It is appropriate for a ninth grader's capabilities for critical thought to be sufficiently developed that a teacher can work directly with them. At this time, healthy students will begin to believe and accept as true only that which they have developed through their own thought processes.

The teacher must act as a guide to help the pupils arrive at conclusions out of their own effort. The teacher's goal is to ask questions that encourage the students to find appropriate answers *out of themselves*. Through such a process the students gain the realization that truth is acquired through understanding and not by "passing on" facts to be memorized. Students educated in this manner will be well prepared to face the world's many challenges. They will have the skills necessary to investigate with awareness new situations that they encounter. They will have the ability to discover relationships and order when encountering the new. Strong conceptual power, brought together with imagination, can form the basis for appropriate responses that are put into action. The students are prepared to confront what was previously not known.

Sense-based science pedagogy is a means to a successful transition between the imaginative wonder of the early grades and the clear, conscious, insightful thinking possible for students of high school age. By learning to understand basic phenomena directly, confidence to face the uncertainty and confusion of early adolescence is won. The sense-based pedagogy described in this book gives students experiences that are fundamental to understanding human perception and cognition. The students are encouraged to begin to make sense of their world. They enter into an understanding not only of the world, but also of how they perceive that world. They engage in questions such as, "What is the basis for human perception of sound? the visual realm? warmth?" Although the phenomena are elementary, the outcome of engaging with them is powerful.

In Waldorf schools, students create their own record of each class through written compositions and artistic illustrations. Making an illustration of a phenomenon or an apparatus develops and enhances observational skills. As such skills develop, students are able to create more detailed and more accurate illustrations. One need only look at the artistic and scientific work of Leonardo da Vinci to appreciate the cognitive possibilities of artistic engagement.

Twelve-year-olds' awareness of the world and of themselves still rests in the percept. By giving students a possibility for discovery, we try to bring them to a greater awareness of the order inherent in many familiar phenomena. They find, for example, simple relationships between the intervals they hear and the length of the vibrating string, between illuminated and nonilluminated objects, or hot and cold ones. They even find relationships between electrical phenomena and magnetic phenomena, even those phenomena that are much more subtle and hard to notice.

In seventh grade somewhat greater complexity is discovered in the relations between phenomena. This is done in a context in which students are encouraged to become more aware of the activity of their own senses. The lawfulness of reflections seen when looking into a pond lends itself to such study. Greater complexity is associated with the impossibility to get physically into reflection space so as to directly measure relations that are obtained. Also, the teacher encourages the beginning of the awareness in the students of the role their senses play in gaining the visual phenomena seen in the pond. Or in mechanics, as an example of increasing complexity, the students and their teacher develop a mathematical formula that can be used to predict how to bring a mechanical balance into equilibrium *before* a test is done. The class derives the formula by thinking about the results of their previous day's activity; it is not passed down as abstract information to be learned.

In the eighth grade, the students are challenged with questions relating to phenomena that require even more subtle understanding: What happens to our visual world at the boundary between two different transparent media? How can we understand thermal radiation? How do we move from understanding the simple electrical deflections of a vane to the development of a modern electromagnetic motor? It is here that teachers are most challenged to help students begin to work mentally with the phenomena in a model-free way to try to find relationships between them.

The method employed in the sense-based curriculum that is described in this book requires of the student little memorization. When a dispute about what happens arises between two students, or a student questions the teacher, it is settled by revisiting the phenomena. There is no dogma regarding experience. Students have their own experience that they try to understand. They usually feel that they have learned something. The student may say, "I will no longer rely on the teacher to tell me what is right or wrong. I can know that from my own experience! I can confirm the correctness of my thinking by comparing it to my own experience."

In an age of specialists and experts, the ability to determine what is right by one's own individual experience is fast becoming rare. Often, genius shows itself through fresh understanding that does not accept habitual ideas taken for granted by others.

By the end of the eighth grade, students should be capable of gaining awareness of exceptional phenomena that are present in a given situation but are often overlooked or have been previously unnoticed. They learn to be conscious of what *they* actually experience, and they are capable of communicating that experience in written or artistic form. Students who are able to do this by the end of eighth grade are well prepared for the more complicated tasks of high school physics.

How to Use This Book

The demonstrations presented in this book are intended to be experienced in a specific sequence out of which cognition will unfold. They are grouped by subject and day. For example, Demonstration 8W1 refers to the first set of experiences in the eighth grade sequence on warmth. It consists of two parts, both to be encountered on the first day. We strongly recommend that teachers try the experiments themselves *prior* to doing them with their students. In this way teachers can experience the phenomena without the pressure of the lesson. A clear perspective that can guide the presentation to the students on the next day is thereby gained. Such a trial can also give the teacher an opportunity to fine-tune the apparatus.

On the day of the actual experience, the class should not talk about possible conceptual understandings of what they experience or of relationships between phenomena. Such conceptual development is intended to be saved for the "Review" on the following day. During the "Review" the students first focus on details of arrangement of any apparatus and on the procedure followed. Then they can share detailed observations. At this time the students should look for relationships between phenomena. They should try to develop relations between individual phenomena in the sense of finding "conditions for appearance." Such explanations should be in terms of what they have experienced instead of hypothetical or virtual entities. This practice encourages the students to develop interest in and love for the world. During the review students should be given enough time and be encouraged to fully develop their ideas. They should ask questions as well as give answers. Sometimes, it is the students' own questioning that allows them to have the deepest understanding. An example of this, taken from the study of refraction in the eighth grade, follows:

Having studied the color and "lifting" phenomena associated with looking through a prism (Demonstration 8V3), the students were asked to draw a scene from their homes as they saw it while looking through prisms. The following day, Sarah came to class filled with frustration and a question. Paraphrased, this is what she said:

Yesterday I started to draw the window in my room while looking through the prism. As I sat there drawing, the colors became fainter and fainter. Finally, they disappeared. Then, slowly, they appeared more and more strongly. But now, they were upside down and were different colors! Why did this happen?

When asked at what time of day she did her drawing, and how long it took her to complete it, Sarah replied that she had worked on it the previous afternoon from 3–5 PM. (Sarah had done her drawing on December 10th in Saratoga Springs, NY.) Slowly the class began to realize that at 3 PM the sun was still up, and her window was brighter than the walls. When she first started drawing, Sarah saw the warm spectrum of colors (red-orange-yellow) just above her windowsill. As the sun slowly set, the contrast between window and walls became slighter. The contrast condition for the warm spectrum was no longer present, and the colors disappeared. By 5 PM, when the sun was down, the wall and the room lit by her lamp were now brighter than the window. These were the conditions for the cool colors (cyan-blue-violet) to appear when a brightness contrast was viewed through a prism. From Sarah's question she and many of her classmates developed a much deeper sensitivity to refraction phenomena.

The physics lessons afford an excellent opportunity for students to develop clarity of presentation, both written and pictorial. Sixth-grade students can be encouraged to carry the precision of their geometry lessons into their physics illustrations. With their study of the great artists of the Renaissance, seventh-

and eighth-grade students can be encouraged to "draw accurately what they see." The level of detail in their illustrations often is indicative of the perceptive capabilities of the students. Even a simple form, such as a beaker, lends itself to an exercise in careful observation. Nearly all the phenomena of elementary school physics are encountered in daily life.

Working with the sense-based methods presented in this book, teachers will find their own perceptual abilities becoming heightened. With an increased level of awareness and consciousness, the teacher will find new relationships in the world that, previously, were unnoticed. This experience readily can become a source of enthusiasm and inspiration for teaching. As new details of the world are noticed and shared with the class, students will sense their teacher's own excitement and become more involved themselves. Individual experiences brought to class discussions as examples of phenomena, whether brought by the teacher or the students, are among the most long-lasting reminders of physics. They support and encourage genuine interest in the world. Furthermore, teachers employing sense-based methods may find that their cognizance of students' strengths and weaknesses will increase, enabling them to better meet the students' needs.

We often use tools to help accomplish goals or to obtain more information about the world. However, the benefits and limitations of each tool must be understood in order to be able to appropriately employ them. Finally, *all* of this experience must be grasped via our senses and formed into a conceptual understanding or an image. For this reason it is imperative that we understand and develop our perceptual faculties in order to benefit wisely from an external tool.

Sixth Grade Physics

Sound – Acoustics	1 week
Visual Experience – Optics	1 week
Warmth and Cold	4 days
Electricity and Magnetism	1 week

SOUND – ACOUSTICS

We begin our study by becoming more aware of different sounds. What are their qualities? What are the conditions necessary for a sound to be heard? After the students have experienced and understood the connection between sound and motion, we help them to find the arithmetic relations between sound and objects that move in connection with what we hear.

DAY 1
Demonstration 6S1. Awareness of Sound

Create an atmosphere of total silence among the students. With eyes closed, silently and with no movement (important!) *LISTEN.* Begin this exercise outside the classroom the first day, and then repeat the exercise in the classroom. What do you hear? Ask the students to describe the qualities of the sounds they hear. Notice any spatial aspects. Create sounds with different materials that are not visible to the students. Have students describe the qualities of each sound and then see if they can identify its source.

DAY 2
Review Demonstration 6S1

Help the students to review the previous day's demonstration. It is important that they realize they must have the intention to hear in order to be aware of sounds or, alternatively, that the sound is so unexpected that it intrudes into consciousness. Ask the students where they have experienced this.

Demonstration 6S2. Sound Heard through Air, Water and Solid Media:

Most people are aware that they hear sounds while immersed in air. This is a common, everyday experience. Experience of sound via a liquid or solid environment is less common. For example, hit a length of copper pipe that is lying on a table while students put their ears to the pipe and the table. [One-half inch copper pipe is available in any hardware store and in the basements of most schools. Have a student cut the pipe to length with a hacksaw.] Drill a hole in the end of the pipe and suspend it by a string so that a portion of its length is in a tank of water. Students can put an ear into the water when the rod is hit. Also, the teacher can ask students to wrap the ends of the string tightly around index

fingers and then insert an index finger into each ear just before the pipe is struck. Repeat these demonstrations with pipes of different lengths and materials. Note that if the rod is touched the sound stops and something is felt.

Homework: Ask students to completely immerse an ear in water, in a bathtub or a large bucket of still water. Then ask them to listen while they knock on a rigid side of the tub or bucket. They should compare this sound to what they hear when they knock on a completely submerged solid object.

DAY 3
Review Demonstration 6S2

Students who have done the "homework" will want to describe many experiences. During the discussion be sure also to encourage students to share other experiences where they have encountered sound in liquid or solid environments. They can describe experiences such as swimming in a pool, or in a lake with power boats, or listening with an ear to a door or to a railroad rail. You can then ask, "Why does a doctor use a stethoscope?"

Note that the sound quality of struck objects depends on factors such as shape, length and material. Emphasize that longer rods result in lower pitch than do shorter ones of the same material. Also, a rod needs to be physically quivering in order to sound. In addition, imperfections in the material such as cracks and chips affect the quality of the sound that is heard. A cracked wine glass or bell will demonstrate this. Ask students what they think the Liberty Bell might sound like.

Demonstration 6S3. Musical Sound:

Invite a few guest musicians to class so that the students can listen to a string quartet or trio. Have students describe the sound and try to connect qualities with individual instruments. *[It is important to start with music in its wholeness. Only after this is done should the parts be introduced, for example, in the form of a monochord. After students can pick out the sound from each instrument have them listen to each instrument individually. What are the different qualities?]*

When finished with the music introduce students to the monochord. A monochord is easily constructed. (Kits are available. See Apparatus and Supplies List and Sources section.) For simplicity it should be made with a string length of exactly one meter or one yard.

First pluck the monochord with an open string. (Do not bow.) Then ask the students to find the octave by changing the length of the string. A narrow rigid wooden bridge that spans the width of the monochord can be employed to change the length of the string. The bridge is notched to slightly lift and support the string. *Students should, on their own, determine the ratio of the string length of the octave relative to the length of the open string.* [1] (Numbers in [ ] brackets indicate a reference, p. 107.)

DAY 4
Review Demonstration 6S3

Ask the students to recall the musical performances from the previous day. What sound quality did they experience listening to the ensemble? Have them compare this to the sound qualities of the instruments played individually. Was there a relationship between the size of an instrument and its sound? Do the students recognize a similar size relationship in their previous experience (with copper rods)?

What did the students discover regarding the string length ratio between octaves? Since this same length ratio is obtained with any string instrument, we can note the law: *Halve the string length to produce an octave. [A scientific law is a statement of conditions necessary for a particular experience.]*

Demonstration 6S4. Musical Intervals:

Ask the students, by sliding the bridge of the monochord, to find several intervals other than the octave—for example, discover a fifth, a third. For each interval they should note the length of the vibrating string that has been plucked. As before, students should themselves find the ratios of the lengths.

The teacher can then complete the work with the monochord with two brief demonstrations. First, bow the monochord string. Next, invert the monochord and place a mixture of fine sand and lycopodium powder on top of the inverted sounding board. [See Apparatus and Supplies List and Sources (ASLS) section.] Then bow across the inverted string. Follow this experience with a single demonstration of a bow drawn across an edge of a Chladni plate on which the same powder and sand mixture has been sprinkled. (Ernst Friedrich Florens Chladni [1756–1827], a physicist at the University of Göttingen and possibly the world's foremost acoustician, designed and built musical instruments based on his studies.)

DAY 5
Review Demonstration 6S4

Begin by reviewing the string length ratios found for various sound intervals. The students can then describe the demonstrations with lycopodium powder/sand mixture spread on the monochord and the Chladni plate. Be sure that the students have recognized the relationship between sound and movement. Movement (often a fine quivering) and sound occur together. Where there is sound there is movement, and where there is movement there is sound. *One does not cause the other.* Sound and movement are experienced together. They are reciprocal. Furthermore, *sprinkling powder on vibrating-sounding structures is not making sound visible!* Such a suggestion would be similar to saying that Beethoven's Symphony No. 9 is equivalent to the patterns seen on an oscilloscope screen when the instrument is connected to a microphone in the concert hall. (We recommend that this issue be discussed in detail in connection with Eighth Grade Physiology lessons concerning the inner ear.)

Demonstration 6S5. Chladni Figures:

The teacher can demonstrate the bowing of Chladni plates of different shapes, size and/or material. The quality of bowing itself will strongly influence the sound and powder/sand figures.

End week with singing.

VISUAL EXPERIENCE – OPTICS

Vision is the predominant human sense. To function in the world we rely on seeing more than any other faculty we possess. Our dependence on seeing is so resolute that we use it to prejudge other sense experience. For example, we expect that a well-formed and richly colored apple will taste sweet. Or we expect that fresh-looking cut flowers will be fragrant but dried flowers won't.

Such strong reliance on visual experience can lead a person to believe that what is seen is what actually exists, without considering the totality of our experience of the world. After all we say, "Seeing is believing." Nevertheless, all visual experience consists only of seeing images (i.e., seeing pictures).

DAY 1

The initial visual experience in the elementary physics course is within a context in which seeing color, brightness and darkness is emphasized while nonvisual qualities are muted.

Demonstration 6V1. Sunrise:

Ideally and very much the best way to start this week is to observe the world scene arise from out of *total darkness* during a sunrise. (To achieve maximum darkness, the moon should be new or waxing. The experience of total darkness is not possible in a modern metropolitan area.) *This encounter is so important and extraordinary for understanding that it is worth the effort to organize the experience.*

Another, although less stunning, approach is to place the students in a *totally dark* room and, in silence, slowly illuminate the environment. (Use a dimmer and a 500-watt light bulb.)

The teacher needs to lead the students' observations during this exercise. Note the first appearance of very faint brightness. The world then becomes visible in varying shades of darkness. As the shade contrast increases, shapes appear; it becomes possible to begin to discern objects and to develop a field of depth. The first colors to appear are the warmer colors (red, orange and yellow). These are followed by cooler colors (cyan, blue and violet). The field of depth greatly becomes much more distinct with the appearance of colors. Notice that the colors themselves change as the brightness changes. When the demonstration is done with a light bulb and dimmer the colors can be seen to "bleach out" if there is sufficiently intense illumination.

DAY 2

Review Demonstration 6V1

Ask the students to describe the relationship between brightness and what they saw. An aspect of this is the realization that the world *appears* in all its spatial, colorful richness when illumination is balanced between lightness and darkness.

In addition to appreciating the relationship between brightness and what we see, it is important that the student recognize that essential conditions for seeing are a human being, an object to be seen, and a luminous body. All three must be present for one to have the experience of a visual picture. For example, outer space is dark—in spite of the presence of the sun and a viewer—because of the absence of an object to be seen.

Demonstration 6V2. Self-Illuminating, Dependently Illuminating, and Self-Dark Bodies:

The experience of true darkness is that of *voidness*, not blackness. To show this, punch open a metal food can with a triangular juice punch. Empty and clean the can. Then spray its interior with flat black paint. Look into the opening in the can and compare this experience with that of looking at a lit lamp. When you look at the lit lamp you see only *brightness. There is no object called light that can be seen. Light cannot be seen in the light bulb. Light cannot be seen traveling from the light fixture to the seen object. Light cannot be seen traveling from the seen object to the human eye.* We see brightness and darkness. In a balance of these two conditions the world of objects appears to the seeing observer. At this juncture we introduce terminology to distinguish between the qualities of visually unlike objects. Lit light bulbs, flames and glowing fireflies are themselves bright. Following von Mackensen's nomenclature, we say they are self-illuminated. In contrast, caves, mineshafts, pupils of human eyes and our flat black paint can are always dark, even when brought near a source of illumination. They are self-dark. Self-dark objects are actually *spaces* surrounded by an object. Finally, there are objects that appear only when in the vicinity of self-illuminated objects. These are dependently illuminated. [2]

DAY 3
Review Demonstration 6V2

Begin class by reviewing the previous day's concepts. Students can give examples of self-illuminated, self-dark and dependently illuminated objects.

Demonstration 6V3. Shadows:

Begin the class by observing shadows out of doors. Note the geometrical relationships between illuminant (self-illuminated), object (dependently illuminated) and shadow. Look at the shadows of finely edged fir trees and notice that the shadows are not the needle shape of the leaves but rather that the bright areas surrounded by shadow are circular discs (the shape of the sun). [The leaves are acting together here as a pinhole camera giving images of the sun. This concept is further discussed in the Seventh Grade Physics *in re* the *camera obscura*.] Observe that there is always a bit of fuzziness at the edge of shadows. Create the conditions for shadows inside the classroom.

The condition for strong, sharp shadows is a strong point-like self-illuminant positioned close to an opaque object. Have students draw a dependently illuminated object exposed from various perspectives to a single self-illuminant. Note that one side is always illumined and one not, thus illustrating the balance of brightness and darkness (day/night). *[As previously stated, light cannot be seen. There are no rays to be seen.]* The above phenomena can be understood in the terms: The surface of objects in a line of sight with a bright body will be bright while those not in a line of sight will be dark.

DAY 4
Review Demonstration 6V3

What conditions necessarily exist for shadows to be seen? What is the relationship between the location, size and shape of a shadow and the surrounding objects and self-illuminated bodies? Note that shadows were found on the side of an object that was the opposite of the side facing a self-illuminated object.

Demonstration 6V4. After-Images:

After-images are always enjoyed by the students. They can be created as follows: Darken the room and gaze for a while out of a small, bright window. Then shift the students' gaze to a dark wall. A contrasting pattern of light and dark is needed. The frames of the glass panes of a window work well. (If necessary, a large pattern can be painted, black upon white, instead of the bright window bordered in darkness. Place the painted pattern on the blackboard. If the blackboard is really black, shift the gaze from pattern to blackboard.) Have students draw what they see.

Then, paint a 5–6"-diameter black disc on a white background. Gaze at the disc. Then shift the students' gaze to the white background. Next paint 5–6"-diameter discs of saturated colors—red, green, blue and yellow—on a white background. Ask the students to gaze at each of the discs in turn. After looking at each disc, shift the students' gaze to the white background. Finally, you might ask students to paint a color wheel. *[We have already noted that visual experience always requires a human being as well as a self-illuminant and an object. In the case of after-images the human being is dominant in the effects. In the previous cases the physical situation was dominant in bringing about the observed effects. Goethe spoke of physical color (effects influenced primarily by conditions of illumination), physiological color (effects influenced primarily by the human observer) and chemical color (effects influenced primarily by the nature of the pigment).]*

DAY 5
Review Demonstration 6V4

What color was experienced as the after-image of each colored disc? After-images have a lawfulness: The after-image of a color is that which appears opposite from the original color on the color wheel. These pairs of colors are said to be *complementary*. Also, black and white are after-image opposites even though they do not appear on the color wheel. [It is the authors' experience that some students do not see the same colors seen by the majority of the class. This is, of course, to be expected of those who are colorblind.]

Demonstration 6V5. Translucent Bodies:

Brightness can be seen through human skin (hold up fingers in front of candle in darkened room—show this phenomenon as depicted by Georges de la Tour in numerous paintings, including his *Young girl at candle time* and his *St. Joseph, carpenter*), very thin leaves, rice paper, snow, many plastics and cloudy ice. Clear images cannot be seen. Images can be seen through transparent bodies (clear ice (water), liquid water, cornea of eye, glass, and air). Translucent bodies have associated shadows that are an intermediate stage between the shadows of transparent and opaque bodies. Demonstrate these effects with translucent and transparent materials.

WARMTH AND COLD

People can survive for a few days without food. They will complain about the lack of water in a matter of hours. They will complain about the lack of air in less than a minute. Most pressing of all is the lack of warmth, which happens almost instantaneously. To realize this, step outside on a very cold wintry day without a coat.

DAY 1
Review Demonstration 6V5

Review how human beings employ the visual sense to learn about the world. 1. Color tells us something about the form of an object. 2. The interplay of brightness and darkness gives us information about the form of the object. Also brightness and darkness are factors that influence the object's color. 3. Shadows tell us something about the depth of an object and/or its distance from the observer. 4. The apparent size of the object gives us clues as to its distance from the observer. [This is an initial indication of perspective. Do not, however, use the word perspective. This understanding can be recalled next year when perspective is studied.]

Demonstrations 6W. Hot and Cold Materials:

Demonstration 6W1a

How do we know how hot or cold something is? We touch it. Pass around a piece of ice. Pass around a cup of hot chocolate or soup. Ask students to touch the tops of their desks. Students should describe all these experiences.

Demonstration 6W1b

Most people only rarely experience liquids that are hotter than boiling water. For this experience, use a cast iron plumber's spoon, some lead-free tin solder (available in a plumbing supply shop) and a Bunsen burner or propane torch. *Use hot mitts.* (These will be needed in later demonstrations, too.) Melt the solder. [The initial demonstration with the tin is to give the students the experience of very hot liquefaction, unlike that of ice to water.]

DANGER! MOLTEN METAL CAN CAUSE SEVERE BURNS. BE VERY CAREFUL. MAKE SURE THE SPOON IS DRY. STUDENTS SHOULD STAND CLEAR AND ALL SHOULD BE WEARING SAFETY GLASSES. Demonstrations with molten metal make powerful impressions on the students but must be done with extreme care and caution. Observe. Skim off the top of the molten metal with an ordinary spoon. Notice the extraordinary mirror surface that is produced. Pour half of the molten metal into a bucket of cold water. Allow time for the remainder to air cool in the plumber's spoon.

Demonstration 6W1c

Pour boiling hot water and ice cold water one at a time into a basin (any material, including plastic, will do). Listen to the difference in sound of the water pouring on itself.

DAY 2
Review Demonstration 6W1

Ask students to order ice, the desk, human body, candle, hot chocolate and molten tin in order of hotness. Let the students talk about how they know this ordering. (Teacher should not yet make a statement regarding this issue.)

Demonstration 6W2a. Melting Ice by Pressure:

For this experience use a block of ice that has been stored at a temperature just below that of freezing, 32°F (0°C). Tie two large weights (10 lbs each) to a thin piece of bare metal wire. A thin

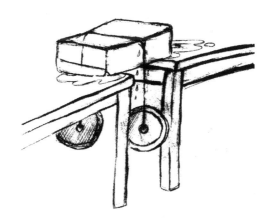

metal guitar string works well. Place the wire across the block of ice so that the weights are freely suspended on either side. Once it is noticed that the wire is beginning to "cut" into the block of ice, begin the following demonstrations while allowing the wire to proceed through the ice.

Demonstration 6W2b. Hotness/Coldness Sensed Relative to Thermal Condition of Human Body:

Fill a bowl with very warm but not burning water. Fill a second bowl with similarly cold water. Fill a third bowl with room temperature water. (This bowl can be filled the night before class and just left in the classroom.) Place the bowl of room temperature water between the other two bowls. Have a student place her left hand in cold water and right hand in hot water. Then, warning the student not to speak out describing what she feels, have her place both hands simultaneously in the bowl of room temperature water. The student will probably be so amazed that other students will want to have the experience. (Students should not talk about the experience until they have all had a chance to have it.)

Demonstration 6W2c. Cold Hands/Warm Hands:

Allow students to submerge their hands in the ice water and hold them there as long as they can possibly stand it. Then have them do an activity such as writing their names. Repeat the experience with hot water.

Observe what happened with the block of ice and wire weighted at either end.

DAY 3
Review Demonstration 6W2

Hold a conversation with the students about what is hot and cold. Start with the question "Is the room hot or cold right now?" On a good day some will find it hot and others cold. *[Hot and cold is relative to our own bodily condition. There is a full discussion of this point and the three bowls experiment Reference (3).]* What is the effect of hot and cold on the human being? Relate this question to the exercise (6W2c) of putting hands in very cold water and trying to write and in hot water and trying to do the same. (Coldness makes things more solid, rigid, contracted, indrawn. Hotness makes things flowing, open, expanded and outward.) Compare the natural posture of someone on a beach during the summer and that of someone waiting for a bus on a wintry February morning. (If the physics lesson is done in the winter, the students can have this experience by going outside without coats.)

Regarding the block of ice (6W2a): Water is unique. Its melting point *drops* with pressure. (Most other materials' melting points rise with pressure. When we talk of the melting temperature of a material, it is usually left unsaid, but atmospheric pressure is assumed.) The weighted wire applied pressure to the ice, which melted locally under the wire and allowed the wire to pass through the melted portion. Once the melt was above the wire the ice was no longer pressurized and therefore refroze because its temperature was again below the melting point (which is higher because of the lower pressure). This temperature, whether the water was solid or liquid, was constant and was equal to that of the surrounding mass of ice. This is the reason that we are able to ice skate. The pressure of the blades reduces the melting point of the water (ice) so that we are able to skate on a layer of liquid, which refreezes after we pass by because of the reasons given above. (The blade acts similarly to the wire.) Discuss with students why skating is so poor when it is extremely cold outside (or cars are then less subject to skids).

Demonstration 6W3. Melting and Boiling Water:

Place a piece of ice into an 800- or 1000ml beaker. Don't use too large a piece of ice because the demonstration will take an inordinately long time to accomplish. Using a Bunsen burner or torch, bring the ice through liquid state to gaseous state (steam). Carefully observe all the changes that occur. Students can draw several of the observed situations. *Students should be absolutely quiet.* Keeping quiet in the room is easier if students are drawing. However, the teacher may need to remark: "I see something new. Does everyone see it?"

DAY 4
Review Demonstration 6W3

Review the observations from Demonstration 6W3. Make sure to note that one kind of bubbling occurred well before boiling. The first bubbling was the release of air that is dissolved in the water. The second kind of bubbling is the release of steam, or boiling.

Demonstration 6W4. Fluid Forms in Hot, Tepid and Cold Water:

Using a fountain pen, let a drop of ink fall into each of three beakers containing ice cold, room temperature and near boiling water. Observe. Again talk about differences between hot and cold water.

[Teacher's note: In this case, we have somewhat removed ourselves from the situation. However, we must always bear in mind that the meaning of hot and cold is always rooted in the human experience of these qualities. By warmth we mean hotness or coldness. Warmth is an inner aspect of the material that speaks to its transformation possibilities. To increase its transformational potential, the warmth of a body usually needs to

be increased. Exposing a colder body to a warmer body does this. For example, the ice was melted (transformed) by being exposed to the hot beaker and hot air within the beaker. The beaker was made hot by being exposed to the hot flame. The air in the beaker was made hot by being exposed to the hot beaker. (This chain of thinking can be taken back as far as the sun and its effects on the leaves of the plants that become the source of fuel.) This image of the transformational possibilities of warming is also portrayed in many myths and legends such as that of the Phoenix rising from the ashes. The baking of bread can be used as another example of the transformational properties of warmth.]

ELECTRICITY AND MAGNETISM

[Important note: The Sixth Grade electricity experiments are centered around Tribo-Electricity (frictional or static electricity). These require very dry air. Therefore, these experiments are best done in Winter (January or February in the Northern

Hemisphere).] If we look and listen carefully, Nature will share some of her secrets with us. Yet, on occasion, out of nowhere, something happens and then is gone. At these times, we must look and listen with even more awareness.

DAY1
Review Demonstration 6W4

These observations can be related to the results of Demonstrations 6W2c.

Demonstration 6E1a. Producing Tribo-Electric Effects: Amber and Rabbit Fur:

Introduce electricity by using a piece of rabbit fur [see ASLS] rubbed with amber (an amber necklace works quite well). Students must be absolutely silent. The room must be silent. Close the windows to cut out noise. Everything must be completely dry, including the teacher's hands. Listen for "crackles." Pull a few hairs from the fur and place them on black construction paper on a table. Rub the amber with the rabbit fur. Slowly bring the amber close to the hairs. Then slowly bring the fur close to the hairs. Experiment with what happens when the hairs touch the amber and the fur; then try to again obtain the original effects. Only after these effects have been well observed, *very* lightly spray the fur with water and repeat. (Note: Amber was the original material with which electrical effects were observed. The Greek word for amber is electron.)

Demonstration 6E1b. Producing Tribo-Electric Effects: Cotton and Contact Paper:

Place an 18" x 24" sheet of contact paper on a table. Have a student hold each corner of the *backing paper* firmly onto the table. *Tear* cotton balls into small wispy pieces and spread them

on the top surface of the contact paper. *Carefully,* lifting evenly in a smooth motion, separate the contact paper from its firmly held down backing sheet. [When separated, the cotton wisps will stand straight up. Some may even jump.] Smoothly and gently move contact paper up and down without touching backing.

Demonstration 6E1c. Producing Tribo-Electric Effects: Glass Rod, Silk Cloth, Pith Ball:

With a thread, hang a pith ball [see ASLS] from a clamp stand. (A pith ball is formed from the spongy growing layer of plants.) Rub a glass rod with silk cloth. Bring the rod near the pith ball, being careful not to touch the pith ball with the rod.

DAY 2
Review Demonstration 6E1

Ask students to describe what they observed. [Note: *They did not hear or see electricity!* They heard crackling; they may have seen sparks. They certainly saw motion (cotton strands stood up,

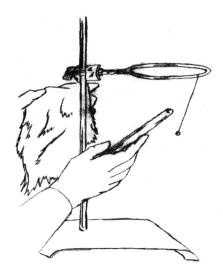

rabbit hairs stood up, pith ball moved), but they did not directly see a "thing" called electricity. By electricity we mean those particular effects that happen under a given set of conditions. For these effects to occur, the materials had to be treated in a special way. They had to be placed in intimate contact and separated. The preparation process creates a state of electrical condition that gives rise to the visual and aural phenomena that were then observed.] What are the material conditions for this effect? Two dissimilar dry materials must be brought into intimate contact and then separated. (Depending upon the materials chosen and the humidity, the effect can be weak or strong.)

Demonstration 6E2. Electrified Rods and the Electroscope:

Rub the glass rod with a silk cloth. Bring the glass rod near a pith ball without rod and ball touching. Observe motion. Now bring the same rod near an electroscope [see ASLS] and see if there are effects. *Touch* the electroscope with the rod, move the rod away. (The electroscope vane moves and remains displaced.) Place a carpet remnant in front of the classroom. Have two students rub their stockinged feet on the carpet and then touch each other's fingertips, tip to tip. Repeat with different combinations of students. Note that effects are different with different socks, size of student and dryness/dampness of skin.

DAY 3
Review Demonstration 6E2 and compare to
Demonstration 6E1

Discuss the experiments with the pith ball and the electro-scope with the students. The vane's moving and returning when in the presence of the electrified rod was similar to the pith ball's moving when in the vicinity of an electrified rod. The new effect is what happened when the electrified rod touched the electroscope and the rod was then removed. Because the vane's displacement did not relax even after the electrified rod is removed, we can conclude that the electroscope's internal apparatus has been electrified. We have discovered a second way to electrify objects: Touch them with an already electrified object. However, note that the active parts of the electroscope are made of metal. This second kind of electrification process works only for some materials, typically metals. Materials for which this type of electrification works well are called conductors. Conductors are materials that easily change their electrical condition while insulators (dielectrics) do not easily change their electrical condition.

Demonstration 6E3a. Magnetism—
Lodestone and Compass:

In a large bucket or tub float a lodestone [see ASLS] on a very light piece of wood or cork, or possibly a coffee can top of the old kind that has a small cylindrical edge on its end. Allow the lodestone to float on the water *undisturbed* and note its orientation. Reorient float and note that it returns to the originally observed position. [Teacher should try the different surfaces of the lodestone to see which gives the strongest effect. In class, start with the strongest effect and then lay the stone on different surfaces and observe.] The end of the stone that points to the North is called the North Pole (of the earth) seeking end of the stone. [We strongly recommend that the teacher talk about the North and South Pole *seeking* ends of the magnet and not the North Pole of the magnet and the South Pole of the magnet. Definitely do not label the ends of the magnet + and -.] Note that there is an angular difference between true North (the position where the axis about which the earth rotates pierces the earth's surface) and magnetic North. This angle is called the magnetic declination. It appears on maps so that one may orient oneself properly with a compass.

Discuss the use of the lodestone in early navigation. Lodestone deposits were originally found in Magnesia. This is where the word magnetism comes from. Introduce the compass as a modern lodestone. Use an ordinary compass. Note that the compass material is steel: iron mixed with a very small amount of carbon. Compare the compass orientation with the lodestone orientation.

Demonstration 6E3b. Magnetizing Steel:

Place a 3ft-long ½"-diameter steel reinforcing rod (rebar) on a protective surface on the floor. Align rod along a North–South direction. Also try to orient the rod according to the inclination of the magnetic field to the surface of the earth. The inclination varies widely from position to position on the earth. An inclinometer can help here, but the information may be available from a local geologist. The reason that we suggest a long length of rebar is that the effect is small. A longer length will magnify the effect. On the other hand, it is harder to effect the magnetization of the longer rod. Sharply hit the end of the rod repeatedly with a short-handled sledge hammer. If the hammer blows on the end are not strong enough hit the rebar along its length. This may require an inclined

support, such as a metal plate supported by an inclined mound of clay. Unsupported, or even with a board support, this process will not work because the rebar will bend. The hammer blows must be very hard. This process is difficult to achieve, but it is *well worth* it because the student actually experiences the preparation and creation of a magnet.

Tie a fine thread to the center of the rod and hang the from clamp stand. Make sure that thread is at the center of the rod and not beyond the base of the clamp stand (or the rod will fall). Observe what happens.

DAY 4
Review Demonstration 6E3

As with electrical phenomena, here we saw motion without observing any apparent cause. That is, we did not see anything applying a force to the magnetic material. The striking played the same role in magnetizing as did separating from intimate contact in electrification. The magnetization, however, is much more stable so as to be more or less permanent. (Note: Electricity and magnetism were thought to be the same phenomenon until the year 1600 when Sir William Gilbert published *De Magnete*.) [*Teacher's note: These two forces interact in electric motors, which are studied in the eighth grade.*]

Demonstration 6E4a. The Effect of Material and Spatial Orientation on Magnetizing:

The only materials that can be permanently magnetized are those containing the elements iron, cobalt or nickel. Try to hit an aluminum rod or a plastic rod to see if the effect obtained with the rebar can be brought about. Also, try to magnetize a piece of unmagnetized rebar that is aligned perpendicularly to N–S (i.e., E–W). Here you should hammer the bar along its length. See in which direction the bar orients, if indeed you are able to magnetize it. (It should align E–W. However, since the effect is so small, it is quite likely that the twist of the thread will be as strong as the magnetic alignment.)

Demonstration 6E4b. The Effect of Temperature on Magnetization:

Magnetize an 18-inch-long 1/8-inch steel rod. Demonstrate the magnetic N–S orientation. Use a propane torch to raise the temperature so that the rod glows cherry red. *[Caution: Use hot mitts, i.e., high-temperature insulating gloves.]* After the rod has cooled, check for a magnetic effect. (If the rod has been sufficiently heated it will be demagnetized.)

DAY 5

Review Demonstration 6E4

A material is magnetized relative to its orientation to the N–S pole axis of the earth. From this we can know in which direction the lodestone was lying in the earth when it was formed. We can imagine magnetizing nails when building an E–W oriented wall.

[Suggestion: You may want to finish sixth-grade physics by trying to create a picture from nature that illustrates the phenomena experienced in this course. For example, the very last remnants of a sunset suggest brightness, darkness and warmth. A waterfall can suggest sound. Electrical and magnetic effects can be suggested by the *aurora borealis*.]

Seventh Grade Physics

WARMTH AND COLD

We use a spoon or ladle to stir a pot of bubbling soup just before serving. The soup is too hot to stir with our fingers (even if our fingers are clean and we would like an excuse to have something to lick). The utensil mediates our experience of the soup that is too hot to touch directly. However, this doesn't always work as planned; the spoon itself may be too hot to touch. Whether it is too hot depends on the mediating material. While a metal spoon might be too hot to touch, it is unlikely that a wooden or ceramic spoon would be. In like fashion, it is the temperature of the handle that we experience directly when we pick up a pot. The pot and handle mediate our experience of the very hot flame.

Different materials also vary greatly in their degree of expansion upon a temperature change.

DAY 1
Review Sixth Grade Warmth-Cold Experiences

Before introducing new material begin the lessons by helping the seventh grade students to recall, vividly, their experiences of warmth from the sixth grade physics classes. These were:

- Human beings feel hot when they touch a hot body, cold when they touch a cold body.

- Our experience of hot and cold, however, is always in reference to the temperature of our own body. For example, when we come in from the cold the room feels very warm, while the same room feels cool after coming out of a warm shower.
- Almost all materials, with the exception of water between zero and four degrees Celsius, expand as their temperature increases and contract as their temperature decreases.

Demonstration 7W1. The Mediating Effect of Materials on Hotness and Coldness:

Part 1. Boil water in a 1000ml beaker. Place two large, equal-sized spoons, one metal, the other wood, in the beaker. Allow the spoons to be immersed in the water for a minute or two. *Without talking among themselves* ask the students to touch each of the spoons in turn. After all students in the class have touched the spoons ask them to describe their experience (i.e., one feels hot, and one doesn't feel hot).

Part 2. Ask the class whether there is a student who would be willing to remove the beaker from the flame barehanded. How about with a glove or hot mitt? (The teacher can then remove the beaker from the flame *with a hot mitt*.)

DAY 2
Review Demonstration 7W1

Ask your students to recall and describe the previous day's demonstration (7W1). "Was anyone surprised that the hotness of the two spoons in the *same* bath of boiling water was different?" They were in the same bath of boiling water and are of approximately the same size. What was different? (The materials.) How does this relate to removing the beaker with the hot mitt? When in contact with hot (or cold) bodies, different materials feel different with regard to hot and cold. Discuss with the class where they have experienced this phenomenon in their lives. (Ex: Touching a metal handle or a wooden one on a cold day, sitting on a vinyl car seat vs. a cloth one in the hot sun, walking at the beach on sand or on grass.)

Demonstration 7W2. Strong Thermal Mediators (Insulators) and Weak Thermal Mediators (Conductors):

Remove the top lids of four metal food cans of the larger size typically used for fruit or tomato sauce. Wash their insides clean. Do the same with four smaller cans, of the size used for canned soup, so that they can be placed inside the larger ones. (Ideally, there should be one-half-inch clearance between the cylindrical surfaces of the cans.) Place sufficient gravel in the bottom of the larger cans so that the tops of both the larger and the smaller cans are at the same height when inserted into one another. (The purpose of the gravel is to act as ballast.) Fill the space in the large can of the first pair with room-temperature water, the second pair with sheared wool, and the third with sand. Leave the fourth pair filled with air. Place the four pairs of cans in a pan of hot water filled to a depth such that the cans are almost covered but don't quite float. Now place equal-size ice cubes in each pair of cans. Observe and keep track of the time it takes for the ice cubes to melt completely.

DAY 3
Review of Demonstration 7W2
What did we observe regarding the time it took for each ice cube to melt? How might this relate to how we might stay cool on a warm day? How about staying warm on a cool day? (The air and the sheared wool isolate the ice cube from effects of the warm water much more than do the water and sand. Note that there is

air "trapped" in the sheared wool.) Materials that isolate from thermal effects across their thickness are called insulators, and those that are thermally transparent are known as conductors. A material that thermally isolates is one that, when touched by a human hand, feels neither hot nor cold even though it is in close contact with a hot or cold body. How does this relate to animals? (For example, the trapped air in sheep's wool and in animal fur.)

Demonstration 7W3. Thermal Expansion of Solids:

Part 1. With a Bunsen burner or propane torch, heat a long thin bolt that is supported in a metal- or glass-fiber clad clamp mounted on a clamp stand. (A four- or five-inch carriage bolt will do fine.) When fully heated, *immediately* measure the length of the bolt with a pair of calipers. Then place the bolt in a bucket of very cold ice water and re-measure its length with the calipers.

Part 2. From the science kit available from Waldorf Publications or from a scientific supply catalog [see ASLS section], obtain a "ball and ring" apparatus. Demonstrate that the ball passes through the ring. With the ball through the ring, heat

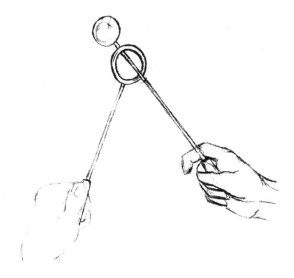

the ball with a torch or Bunsen burner. Try to pull the ball back through the ring. (The ball will not pass through the ring.) Now, heat the ring so that the ball easily passes back through it. Next, place the ball through the ring again and reheat the ball so that it does not pass through the ring. This time, immerse the ball in a bucket of cold water and then pass it back through the ring.

DAY 4
Review Demonstration 7W3

All solid materials expand when heated and contract when cooled. This is of great importance technologically. For example, consider expansion joints on bridges where metal fingers mesh between sections of pavement: The fingers are more closed in the summer and more open in the winter. Even small highway bridges are constructed with a gap between the road pavement and the bridge pavement. The bridge is constructed with a substructure that allows its pavement to expand and contract on steel rollers.

The space shuttle experienced problems because the thermal insulation tiles expanded at a slower rate than did the underlying metal structure of the shuttle. To solve this problem, engineers used a special adhesive that allowed the ceramic and metal substructure to expand and contract independently. Historically, the pendulums of clocks were constructed with assemblies of different metals so that when one metal expanded in hot weather another metal expanded in the opposite direction to keep the length of the pendulum constant (and the time accurate).

Demonstration 7W4a. Thermal Expansion and Contraction of Liquid Water:

Completely fill a flask with water and fit with a one-hole stopper and a 2ft length of glass tubing. Heat the flask. Observe the level of water in the glass tube. (If you wish, the water can be colored with vegetable dye, litmus or copper sulfate solution.) Let the flask cool, and observe. When the flask is cool to the touch, it can be cooled with an ice bath. (Danger! Do not cool the hot flask with the ice bath. The glass may crack.)

Demonstration 7W4b. Thermal Expansion and Contraction of Air:

Obtain a thin-walled metal can such as those in which maple syrup or olive oil is sometimes packed, or a new UNUSED (!) gasoline can (remember "thin walled") that can be purchased in most hardware stores. Using detergent and hot water carefully clean the remnants of olive oil and maple syrup. (Danger! Even a "cleaned" previously used gasoline can is an extreme explosion hazard. DO NOT USE!) An airtight seal is required. Place the can on a ring stand and heat as much as possible. Use hot mitts. Remove the burner and immediately seal the can. A close-fitting rubber stopper will work. Allow the can to cool. (The walls of the can will "bow" in, often accompanied by audible "pops.") With the classroom very quiet, remove the stopper from the can.

DAY 5
Review of Demonstration 7W4
These demonstrations illustrated that materials expand when their temperatures are raised and contract when their temperatures are lowered. In Demonstration 7W4a, the liquid water expanded and rose up the narrow tube. Since the amount of expansion corresponds to how hot the liquid feels to the touch, we can relate the height of the water column to the hotness of the water. This is the basis of a thermometer. Note also that the glass expands. This means that as the glass gets hot the volume of the flask and the diameter of the tube increase. But since the rate of expansion of glass is much less than that of water, the increase in the volume of the glass tube is extremely small and can be neglected. Therefore, the height of the water column can be used

as an indication of temperature. Note: This primitive thermometer is open to the atmosphere and will give lower readings if the barometric (atmospheric) pressure is high and pushes down on the water column. Gases expand and contract much more than do liquids or solids.

In Demonstration 7W4b, the sealed container was filled with hot air that, upon cooling, had a very strong impetus to contract. Such contraction reduced the pressure inside the can. Since the atmospheric pressure (i.e., the air pressure outside the can) was now greater than the air pressure inside the can, the walls of the can were pushed in by this imbalance of force. The air in the can now occupied a smaller volume. Upon removing the stopper from the can after cooling, air could be heard to rush in, showing that the air in the can must have been at lower pressure than that of the atmosphere.

VISUAL EXPERIENCE – OPTICS:

The focus of the sixth-grade work was the relationship of brightness and darkness to the visual scene. The seventh-grade emphasis is on spatial relationships between images, particularly those between images in the tangible world and those in reflection space.

DAY 1
Demonstration 7V1. Reflection in a Natural Pond (or a Puddle on Pavement):

Take the class to a still body of water, ideally a natural pond. If a natural pond is not available, even a puddle on a city street will work. Carefully observe the images within the boundary of the water. Be sure the students move around the body of water. (They should see that the scene changes according to their point of view.) The students should sketch the scene *as they actually see it* within the frame of the water.

DAY 2
Review Demonstration 7V1

What was seen? A scene that mirrors the visual world above the water's surface, the bottom of the pond, leaves floating on the surface, perhaps fish or reeds in the water itself. Colors in the water's reflected picture are usually somewhat duller than those of their corresponding image (i.e., the usual seen world) above the surface. A still pond (windless day) and a somewhat dark bottom are required for reflections. "Are there any relationships between the visual world of the pond and the images of the world above the pond?" (This question is key for the week's lessons.)

Demonstration 7V2. Reflection in Solids:

Look for images within the frame of a rough piece of metal and a very polished piece of metal of the same material. Aluminum or steel will suffice, or an old chrome hubcap. Try the same with rough and polished pieces of wood. Here it is important that at least one pair of rough and polished wood be of a dark variety like walnut, ebony or mahogany.

Give each student a piece of glass to look in at various angles. The students should note the conditions under which they see reflected images. Repeat the observations with varied backgrounds. For example, the back surface of the glass can be covered with dark or light paper.

DAY 3
Review Demonstration 7V2

Polished surfaces very much enhance the clarity of reflections. Dark surfaces tend to do the same. Relate this to the observations at the pond (7V1). [Note to the teacher: You may want to talk about the history of the mirror. Reflections were first experienced in a body of water. The first mirrors were made by polishing metal. A more modern glass mirror was made by precipitating silver from a silver salt solution onto a piece of glass. The glass protected the silver from being scratched and oxidized. Remember the molten tin from last year? When first formed it produced an extraordinary image. However, this image quickly deteriorated as the tin surface oxidized. The very smooth finish on glass sheets was made by floating molten glass on top of molten metal (float glass) and allowing the glass to cool. (Glass solidifies at a higher temperature than does metal.)]

Demonstration 7V3. Mirror Image Geometry:

Arrange the class so that the students are standing in a line in front of a very large mirror. (It will probably be necessary to divide the class into groups.) Place a small "x" at eye level on the mirror with a piece of tape. While they are looking at the "x," ask students to describe which classmates they see at the "x." (The students at opposite sides of the line will see each other while the students at the middle will see themselves.) Tape the middle of a

25ft-long piece of string to the "x." Have one student take an end of the piece of string, pull it taut, and sight along its length to the "x." Have another student take the other end of the piece of string, pull it taut, and position herself so that the first student can be seen when she also sights along the edge of the string. [Note! Two perfectly straight strings will be seen extending into the mirror space. Have a third student measure the angle between each string and the surface of the mirror. These angles will be very close to equal. Repeat the measurement with different pairs of students at different positions.]

DAY 4
Review Demonstration 7V3

There was a visually seamless boundary between the reflected space seen within the mirror and the space of tangible objects seen outside the mirror. When looking into a mirror along a particular line of sight (at a particular angle to the surface of the mirror), a visual image within the mirror space appeared along that same line of sight. (The string did not have a bend in it at the mirror surface.) For an observer directly opposite the "x," the line of sight from observer to her own (corresponding) image was perpendicular. Also, the "reflected observers" seen in the mirror space directly across from the actual observers "saw" from within the mirror space to the people in ordinary space along a straight line of sight, just as the actual observers looked into the mirror space and saw the reflected observers. This was illustrated by the straight strings (that connect the "reflected observers" with the observers in ordinary space) seen emerging from the mirror space into ordinary space. The angle between the two observed straight strings and the mirror surface was the same.

Demonstration 7V4. Shadows in Reflection Space:

Place a mirror no smaller than 4" x 6" so that it is perpendicular to the table top. Place a candle approximately six inches from the mirror surface. Place a small opaque object (an unlit candle or a pen cap) between the candle and the mirror and slightly to one side. Carry out this demonstration in an otherwise unlit room. [Unless the room is fairly dark it may not be possible to see a shadow that extends on the table back from the opaque object (i.e., away from the mirror)]. Observe the images and shadows within and without the mirror space. The students should draw what they see.

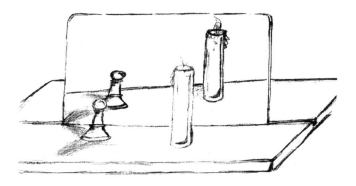

DAY 5
Review Demonstration 7V4

Discuss the observations from the previous day's demonstration. Note the shadow on the table that extended from the mirror and was apparently cast by the reflected candle into ordinary space! Also note the shadow that extended back from the opaque object and was apparently cast from the reflected candle.

Demonstration 7V5. The Camera Obscura:

[This experiment must be set up the night before class. It takes a long time to set up but is well worth the effort. Ideally the room has lightly colored walls, is located on the first floor of the building and has a street scene outside the window. It is easier to darken a small room.]

Completely (!) darken a room by covering all windows, edges of doorframes, etc., with heavy opaque material. (Heavy paper, dense cloth, cardboard, etc.) During daylight of the day previous to the demonstration check for any and all bright spots and cover them so that they are dark. *The darker the room the stronger the image and the more powerful the experience will be for the students (and the teacher!).* In the center of a window, and approximately one foot above the sill, carefully cut a *crisp*-edged circular hole the diameter of a pencil in the covering. Tape a piece of opaque paper over the hole. Set up a large sheet of white paper parallel to the window and about two feet from the hole.

Turn off the lights and *wait a number of minutes* so that your eyes can adjust to the darkness of the room. Remove the paper cover from the hole. Observe the image on the surface of the white sheet of paper that faces the window. [An inverted image of the outside scene will appear. This phenomenon is known as a *camera obscura*.] As the paper is moved back the size of the image increases. Upon removing the paper completely, the image will be found on the walls, floor and ceiling of the room. (An especially fine experience occurs when a sunset is viewed.)

While others are observing the *camera obscura* image, a few students can be sent outside to move through the scene. Finally, the diameter of the hole slowly can be increased and the effect on the qualities of the image can be observed. (The image becomes brighter but quickly becomes very fuzzy.) Seventh grade students, when experiencing this demonstration, have often exclaimed: "This is better than TV."

[Remind students to bring to class tomorrow a cylindrical metal coffee can or a cardboard oatmeal container and a heavy rubber band.]

DAY 6
Review Demonstration 7V5

Students can describe their experiences of the *camera obscura*. They will have abundant observations. Note that a straight line of sight related corresponding points of the outside image with the inside image and that all of these lines of sight passed through the single point of the hole in the window covering (provided the hole is small and sharp). This is the same phenomenon as that of the images of the sun found on the floor of a heavily canopied forest (See Demonstration 6V3) and is the basis of the pinhole camera (whose construction is described in Project 7V6).

Project 7V6. Constructing a Pinhole Camera:

Students should have brought to school a coffee can or a cylindrical cardboard oatmeal container and a heavy rubber band. Line the inside (sides and bottom) of the container with black construction paper. Punch a finishing nail-sized hole (approximately 1/32" dia.) through the center of the bottom of the container. Cover the open top of the container with waxed or tissue paper secured around the cylindrical edge with the rubber

band. Covering their heads and shoulders with a heavy coat or blanket (similar to the old-fashioned photographers with their view cameras) students can observe the world on their waxed screen via the nail hole. It helps to look at a scene with good contrast between bright and dark objects, and it may be necessary to tightly wrap their jackets about themselves. Also, allow some time for adjustment of eyes to dim illumination. It is often practical to insert the cylindrical box into a closely fitting coat sleeve.

ELECTRICAL PHENOMENA

In the sixth grade, electrical experience was gained when *dry* materials in intimate contact were separated. In the seventh grade, electrical phenomena are generated under *wet* conditions.

DAY 1
Review Visual Experience—Optics
Before beginning electrical phenomena, guide the class to develop a brief summary of imaging via reflection and *camera obscura.*

Demonstration 7E1 The Human Mouth as a Source of Wet-Cell Electrical Activity:

Part 1. Give a fresh, clean pair of copper and zinc strips (approx. 1" x 4") to each student [see ASLS]. Be sure the metal is not heavily oxidized. The metal strips should be shiny. Ask the students to hold one end of a pair of strips together between the thumb and forefinger of one hand and, with the unclamped end, pinch various parts of their skin, fingers, arms, etc. They will be using the pair of strips like a clothespin. [*Teacher's note: Nothing happens, other than pinching. This is to show that something special happens when they do this with the tongue.*] Then, have one of the

students place one metal strip on top of his tongue and the other on the bottom while still clamping the strips together at other end with his fingers. After a few students have done this individually the remainder of the class can have the experience.

Part 2. Using alligator clips, connect a wire lead (2–3 ft in length) to a copper strip and another wire lead to a zinc strip. Have a student place the strips on top and bottom of tongue as before, but this time without clamping the ends together. In other words, this time the two metal strips are not in contact with each other. The teacher or another student can then hold the unclamped ends of the wire leads and alternately touch them together and pull them apart to make and break contact.

Part 3. To each of two wire leads, attach a copper strip to one side of the lead and a zinc strip to the other. Two students can now place one pair of copper-zinc strips in their mouth while being connected with leads to another student. (The effect will probably be stronger.) Additional students can be added to the chain provided that each lead has a copper strip at one end *and* a zinc strip at the other and each student has only a copper-zinc pair on their tongue. (Note: No effect is felt unless all students have a pair of strips in contact with their tongue and all strips are connected to a strip of dissimilar metal. You will quickly discover that a circle is the best form in which to try this experience.)

Finally, have two students, each with a dissimilar pair of strips on his or her tongue, connect leads from copper strip to copper strip and zinc strip to zinc strip.

DAY 2
Review Demonstration 7E1

After students share their experiences make sure that the following essentials have been noted:

- There was no experience until a pair of dissimilar metal strips contacted a wet tongue.
- There was no effect without a complete loop of alternating copper and zinc strips.

Demonstration 7E2. Wet-Cell Battery:

Dissolve salt into 1.5 liters of water to make a saturated solution. (Dissolve as much salt as possible without leaving a residue on the bottom. Initially, larger quantities can be added. But later add only small quantities to prevent a larger residue from being undissolved.) Pour the saturated salt solution into a 400ml beaker so that beaker is aboutthree quarters full. Place a pair of copper and zinc strips partially in this solution, making sure that they are not touching each other. Attach a wire lead to the exposed end of each strip. Students can then touch the ends of the leads to their tongues.

Prepare a number of beakers similarly and connect the leads, alternating between copper and zinc. Do not connect the copper and zinc strips in the same beaker together. Rather, connect a copper strip in one beaker to a zinc strip in another, to form a kind of chain. Leave the last copper-zinc pair unconnected but attach an open lead to each strip. Touch the two open lead ends to a tongue.

DAY 3
Review Demonstration 7E2

The tongue sensed the electrical effect in this case but now is not part of the condition for electricity. [Note to teacher: The archetypal electrical phenomenon is the experience of motion occurring without any material causal agent pushing or pulling the object (i.e., the pith ball) that begins to move. Other phenomena associated with existence of the electrical condition are sparks, crackling sounds, and shocks. In the case of our simple battery (Demonstration 7E2), we have not shown that the effect is electrical. In order to do this, a very powerful battery would need to be constructed, a battery so powerful that pith balls would be attracted to its terminals. The taste experience is merely an additional aspect of the possibilities that occur when the electrical condition is manifested. It is not a demonstration for which the effect is similar to that of the pith balls.] In this case the beakers of salt water, with their pairs of dissimilar metals, constitute the condition for electrical effects to occur. The dissimilar metal strips in the salt water solution or in the saliva constitute a wet-cell battery. Increasing the number of cells and connecting them in alternating fashion increases the strength of the electrical effect. An automobile battery is a wet-cell.

Demonstration 7E3. A Voltaic Pile:

Prepare one liter of saturated salt water solution. Soak strips of filter paper that are the same size as the metal strips in the salt water solution. (The filter paper strips can be cut to size.) Stack alternating strips of copper—zinc—filter paper—copper—zinc— filter paper to obtain a sandwich of five layers of each material.

Stack at the edge of a nonmetallic plate such as glass so that leads can be attached to the bottom (copper) and the top (zinc) plates. Touch the leads to the tongue. Touch the leads to the center post and threaded metal case of the base of a small flashlight bulb.

DAY 4
Review Demonstration 7E3

The "sandwiches" are called voltaic piles. The situation is analogous to the configuration of Demonstration 7E2. The great advantage of the pile is that the space occupied by the battery is greatly reduced. [The Italian Count, Alessandro Volta, first assembled the voltaic pile at the beginning of the 19th century.]

Demonstration 7E4. Expansion, Glowing and Melting of an Electrified Wire:

AUTOMOBILE BATTERIES CAN BE VERY DANGEROUS. FOLLOW DIRECTIONS EXACTLY AS DESCRIBED. This demonstration should be done out of doors and with students wearing safety glasses. Students should NOT touch any wires, including with their tongues.

Attach jumper cables to each end of a 3ft length of 22-gauge (.025" diameter) wire. (A higher gauge number—i.e., *smaller* diameter wire—can be used if necessary.) Drape the wire across two clamp stands supported by metal clamps. (The wire need not be clamped.) Using leather gloves, attach jumper cables to the terminals of an automobile battery. (Note: The wire will expand, glow and melt in approximately 5 seconds. If the wire does not melt within 8 seconds, immediately disconnect the jumper cables from the battery.)

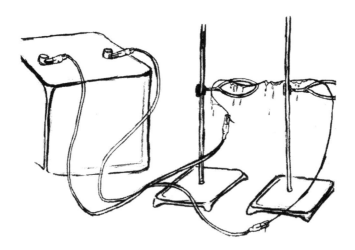

MECHANICS

The ability to lift a heavy object is related not only to the object but also to our own bodies. In addition to strength, the size, limb length and positioning of our body directly influences our success in moving objects from one place to another. The seventh-grade mechanics introduces the concepts of levers, torque and balance to the students via the study of their bodies as well as of machines.

DAY 1
Review Demonstration 7E4

The drooping of the wire showed its expansion. The wire's expansion, glowing and melting all indicated that the wire was at a high temperature. What was different in this situation, compared to the earlier demonstrations with wires and batteries, that such high temperatures were achieved? The battery is very strong. But this is not sufficient. The high temperature was achieved by the combination of a strong battery with a very small diameter wire completing the loop. This is the combination that is used in an incandescent light bulb. (It took Edison a long time to find a material that would not melt. The first successful Edison light bulbs were made with carbon fiber filaments produced by burning plant material. They can still be seen at Edison's workshop in East Orange, New Jersey, which is open to the public.)

Demonstration 7M1. Balance and the Seesaw:

If your school playground has a seesaw, start with that. Otherwise, mark the center of an 8ft x 4" x 4" wood beam (without knots!) and center it across a sturdy saw horse (or substitute such as a large diameter log). (The saw horse must be strong enough to support 400 pounds.) Choose two students of approximately

equal size (weight) to sit at the opposite ends of the beam. Ask the students to then lift their legs from the ground and note what happens. (If the students' weights are close to equal the beam will not move.) Now replace one of the students with a much smaller (or larger) student and see what happens. (Caution students about not lifting their legs from the ground too quickly.) Move the beam from its center and find the point where the beam is balanced with the two students of unequal weight. Also, this can be repeated with two students at one end and only one student at the other. Again, find the position where the beam is balanced.

DAY 2
Review Demonstration 7M1

What happened when two students of equal weight were on a seesaw? What do people on a seesaw do when their weights are not equal? (The smaller person may push harder, lean back, or ask the larger person either to lean forward or, even better, move forward on the beam.) Here, the terminology of the support point about which the beam pivots as the *fulcrum* can be introduced. We see a pattern: Balance is maintained by reducing the distance to the fulcrum of the heavier student and increasing the distance of the lighter student. This distance, from the weight to the fulcrum, is called a *lever arm* or *moment arm*.

Demonstration 7M2. Law of Rotational Balance (Equilibrium):

Prior to class prepare a series of free weights (a selection of 2.5–35 lb. weights of the disc type that are added to a weight lifting bar) with a loop of strong cable inserted through the center hole of the weights. The loop should be large enough so that the weights can hang freely from the beam and move easily along its length. The ends of the cable loop can be connected by tying a knot or using cable connectors (available in a hardware store or from a telephone company employee). While a student holds the beam steady, place a ten-pound weight near the end of the beam. Measure the length of its lever (moment) arm. Place a second ten-pound weight on the opposite side so that the beam is in balance. Measure its lever (moment) arm. (The two will be approximately the same.) Add an additional 10-pound weight to one side (or replace one of the ten-pound weights with a twenty-pound weight) and find the new balance point by moving the larger set of weights. Measure the new lever (moment) arm. Repeat with various combinations of weight placed together at single positions on either side of the beam and recording the weights and lever arms.

DAY 3
Review Demonstration 7M2
The goal of yesterday's exercise was to arrive at an equilibrium relationship, so that when the beam is in balance the product of the weight and its lever arm distance on one side of the beam is equal to the same product on the other side. Expressed as an equation:

$$W^1 \times l^1 = W^2 \times l^2$$

Carry out several calculations where two weights and one lever arm are given and the second lever arm is calculated, or where two lever arms and one weight are given and the second weight is calculated. Use weights and lengths that relate to those used in Demonstration 7M2 so that the calculations can be checked with yesterday's experience.

Demonstration 7M3. Levers and Fulcrums:

Part 1. Place several weights weighing approximately 75 lbs. at an end of the beam with the fulcrum positioned at the beam's center. Ask a student to lift the weights by pushing down on the other end of the beam. Now, slide the weights halfway toward the fulcrum and again have the student lift them by pushing on the opposite end. Is this more or less difficult than the previous effort? Now, with the weights at the end of the beam, move the fulcrum so that the beam is supported at a position about one quarter of its length (two feet) from the weighted end. How does the effort compare to the other two endeavors? Repeat once more, this time with the fulcrum moved toward the end so that it is equidistant from the beam end and the previous fulcrum position (i.e., one foot from the end). Finally, position the fulcrum at the end and place the weights on the same side of the beam as the "lifter."

Part 2. Using a crow bar or a 4- to 6-ft steel pipe or bar, move very heavy objects such as rocks, logs, cast iron stoves, bathtubs, etc. (Keep students away from colleague's automobiles.) Experiment with using different fulcrum positions. (A piece of hard wood works well as a fulcrum.)

DAY 4
Review Demonstration 7M3
Review how the strenuousness of the effort varied as the lever arms changed. Note that as the fulcrum was moved to make the load easier to lift, the amount of lifting of the object decreased, with a given amount of movement of the lever. Thus, for a given effort:

Greater weight lifted <=> smaller distance lifted
Greater distance lifted <=> smaller weight lifted

Use the equation (Demonstration 7M2) to calculate how much push was exerted in each of several cases. (Now, through calculation we have obtained results that we could not otherwise have gotten via measurement without special apparatus.)

Demonstration 7M4a. Changing an Automobile Tire Requires Torque:

Change an automobile tire. Using a 1/4"-drive socket wrench and appropriate socket for the automobile's lug nut, ask one of the stronger students to loosen one of the lug nuts. (You may not be able to find a lug nut socket for a 1/4" drive. In that case use an adapter available at any hardware store or automotive supply store.) He/she will probably not be successful. Try the same with a 3/8"-drive socket wrench (the handle will be longer than that of the 1/4" wrench.) Again, the student will probably not be successful. Now try the same with a 1/2"-drive socket wrench (with an even longer handle). Use a 1/2" socket or an adapter. Try the same experiment with the tire iron that comes with the car. (In this case the student may be able to loosen the nut.)

Finally, on the remaining nuts, use a breaker bar or slip a 4–6ft steel pipe over the tire iron. (Available in hardware and automotive supply stores, breaker bars usually have a 1/2" drive at the end of a long handle. They are used to loosen seized nuts.) Using a scissors jack raise the car. *Use the proper procedures for jacking the automobile as described in the owner's manual.* Remove the wheel and then replace it. (Students should not do final tightening of the lug nuts. Teacher should use a torque wrench to tighten lug nuts.)

Demonstration 7M4b. Arm Wrestle with Socket Wrenches:

Fit a 1/2"-drive socket wrench with a 1/2" to 3/8" adapter. Fit the adapter with a six-inch 3/8"-drive extension. Finally, connect the extension to a 3/8"-drive wrench with a 3/8" socket. Place the extension that is connecting the two socket wrenches on and parallel to the support beam of a saw horse. With the wrench handles on either side of the saw horse support beam, ask two students to have a mechanical version of an arm wrestle.

DAY 5
Review Demonstration 7M4

Discuss the different uses of lever action: Different lengths of lug wrench handles, lever action of the jack (on one side of the car as opposite wheels act as a fulcrum), lever action of the jack handle (whether hydraulic or mechanical), lever action of the different handle lengths in the wrench wrestle. The product of force applied and the length of lever arm is called *torque* or, equivalently, *moment*. In the equilibrium equation the products W_1l_1 and W_2l_2 are magnitudes of torque or moment. The equation of rotational balance or equilibrium can thus be thought of as the concept that the opposite torques are equal when the seesaw is balanced, (i.e., it is in equilibrium).

Demonstration 7M5. Bicycles as Torque Transmitters:

Examine a multi-speed bicycle (minimum 10 speeds) for applications of the use of levers and the concept of torque: Brake levers are long while the lever arm of the brake pad is short. The quick release mechanism for removing the wheels employs a lever. The rear wheel is a lever driven by the chain near the hub. The pedals are attached to the end of a crank (which acts as a lever). Both by riding the bicycle and by turning it over on its bars and seat, various combinations of gears—both front (at the crank) and back (at the rear wheel hub)—can be experienced. Notice the effort required and the resultant speed of the wheel.

DAY 6
Review Demonstration 7M5

Begin by having the students describe the mechanical advantages gained by the many uses of levers (lever arms) on a bicycle. Which gear combinations required the greatest effort, which the least? Which gear combinations produced the greatest speed, which the least? Starting at the crank, the distance from the pedal to the crank axle, along with the push of the leg, determines the torque applied to the axle. (The factor that limits the length of the crank arm is the distance to the ground when leaning into a turn.)

This torque is transmitted to the chain via the selected gear at the crank. The larger the gear, the larger the lever arm, and the smaller the force applied to the chain so that the torque output equals the torque input from the pedals. The larger gears are used on straightaways and downhill where speed is desired and climbing power is not. The lever arm of the smaller gears at the crank is small so that the force on the chain is large in order for the torque output to equal the torque input. Small crank gears are used for hill climbing power. At the rear wheel this is reversed. The force of the chain on a large gear (large lever arm) produces a greater torque than the same chain force would produce on a small gear (small lever arm).

In all cases, the force between the wheel and the road is small because the radius of the wheel (lever arm) is so much larger than the radii of the rear gears. Because smaller gears rotate faster than larger ones for a single rotation of the crank, they result in higher speed. In general, faster speeds are gained at the expense of less torque and vice versa. High torque is needed to climb hills or overcome large headwinds. On a rough rugged course, are larger or smaller wheels more desirable? What about a smooth course?

Eighth Grade Physics

WARMTH – THERMAL PHYSICS

DAY 1
Repeat Demonstration 6W4

The eighth-grade physics lessons begin with a study of movement in relation to the warming and cooling of liquid materials. These phenomena occur all the time in the world around us.

Demonstration 8W1. Warm Air Rises:

Part 1. Build a large fire (outside!). Hold a pinwheel horizontally over the fire. Throw some dry leaves and pieces of newsprint into the fire. Also, ask students to note the experience of the parts of their bodies that are exposed to the fire being very hot while the parts that are not exposed are cold.

Part 2. Find incense sticks that produce a lot of smoke. (In the Orient these are called punk sticks.) Lighting three in a bundle (to obtain a fair amount of smoke), bring the burning bundle of smoke-producing sticks near a hot toaster, a candle, a beaker of ice supported on a ring stand, an open food freezer and a closed window. On a windless, cold day, open the bottom window and

hold the smoking incense bundle at the bottom of the opening and then at the top of the opening. [*Teacher's note: On a sufficiently cold day the smoke from the sticks held at the bottom of the opening will "fall" to the floor inside the classroom and from the sticks held at the top of the opening will rise in the outside air.*]

DAY 2
Review Demonstration 8W1

The spinning pinwheel and the rising bits of newsprint showed that *hotter air rises* (hotter than the surroundings). Driven by the hotter air, smoke particles rise when brought near objects that are warmer than the surrounding environment and fall when brought near objects that are cooler than the surrounding environment. "Where do we ordinarily experience this phenomenon in our daily lives?" Smoke from a fire always rises (although it may also be blown sideways). In the winter the air near the ceiling is hotter than the air at floor level. This is the basis of using ceiling fans (to drive the hot air back down) for more efficient heating, particularly in high-ceilinged rooms like auditoriums. [The teacher may also want to discuss the hot air above a toaster. In this context recall Demonstration 7E4. (The hot wires in the toaster are made of nichrome, a metal alloy with very high electrical resistance and, as well, a high melting temperature.)] The smoke at the bottom of the open window showed that *colder air falls.* At the top the smoke was carried by the hot air from the room rising into the atmosphere.

Demonstration 8W2. Mixing Hot and Cold Liquids:

Using two identical Mason jars, completely fill one to its top with very hot strongly colored tea (Red Zinger works nicely because of its red color) or ink, and completely fill the other jar with clear cold water. **Wearing hot mitts**, cover the jar of hot tea with a rigid *thin* piece of plastic (the top of a 32oz yogurt container with the rim cut away works well) and slowly and carefully turn the jar over and place it (inverted) onto and matching the mouth of the jar with the cold water. Carefully remove the plastic from between the two jars. (Do not be concerned if there is a bit of spillage.) Slide the plastic separator back between the two jars and carefully remove the jar of hot tea to place it right side up on the table. Now cover the jar of cold clear water with the plastic, invert and repeat the procedure. [*Practice this procedure a few times before demonstrating it to the class.*]

DAY 3
Review Demonstration 8W2
There was no mixing when the hot tea was placed over the cold water, while dramatic mixing occurred when the cold water was placed over the hot tea. Hotter liquids rise and colder liquids fall (as do hotter and colder gases). Relate this concept to thermal currents in the ocean (liquids) and thermal currents in the air, both of which very strongly affect the weather. The ocean currents can be understood by considering the George Banks, off the coast of the Maritime Provinces of Canada. As icebergs float south out of the Northern Atlantic Ocean, they begin to melt. The near-ice-temperature meltwater is more dense than the warmer ocean water, and it falls to the ocean floor. Warmer, less dense water rises to the surface. This movement of water stirs the ocean

water and carries sediment rich in minerals to the upper levels of the ocean. Small forms of life thrive on the rich sediments. These smaller forms of life are themselves food for small fish, then larger fish, etc. The George Banks have historically been an important area for fishermen from the East Coast of North America.

The air currents that occur at the beach on hot summer days and cool summer nights can also be discussed. The conditions that create the yearly monsoon in South East Asia also illustrate convection currents.

Demonstration and Discussion 8W3. Warming by Indirect Exposure to a Hot Body:

If possible, arrange for half the students to wear white shirts to class and the other half black ones. Tee shirts will do. On a sunny day the students can describe and share their experiences of warmth when exposed to the sun.

Recall the experience (Demonstration 8W1, Part 1) of portions of the students' bodies that are facing the fire being hot and those not facing the fire being cold. This same experience can be had walking on a sunny cold day in winter. The cheek that is exposed to the sun will be hot while the unexposed one is cold. In these cases warming occurs not by contact with a hot material but by direct exposure to a hot body at a distance. In both examples the surrounding air with which the body is in contact is cold. Nevertheless, the body part that is exposed to the fire or the sun gets hot.

People feel cooler wearing a white shirt on a sunny day than wearing a black shirt. Similarly, black cars are warmer in winter and hotter in summer than are white ones. These experiences illustrate that color affects warming under circumstances of radiation.

[Teacher's note: When bodies get hot by being exposed to a hotter body without physical contact the process is commonly known

as radiation. When bodies get hot by being in physical contact with a hotter body the process is commonly known as conduction. When fluids move because of a relative difference in hotness or coolness the process is commonly known as convection. These terms are universal. However, they seem to imply transfer of an unexperience-able something (called heat) and, to that extent, are problematic for a phenomena-based science. Phenomenological science strives to bring concepts and experience together, rather than create a hypothetical world behind experiences.]

VISUAL PHENOMENA – REFRACTION

In the sixth grade visual experience was considered in relation to tangible objects. The seventh-grade lessons were concerned with the visual experience obtained by looking through smooth surfaces of objects into reflection space. Now, in the eighth grade, students look through the air into a body of liquid or through a transparent solid to view objects in the material on the other side of the air/liquid or air/solid interfaces. Unlike visual objects in reflection space, it is now possible to reach into the visual spaces of the objects to touch them as well as to see them.

DAY 1
Review Demonstration 8W3
"Where have you encountered the various warmth experiences?" (See Demonstration 8W3 for a complete discussion.)

Demonstration 8V1. Refraction Phenomena:

Part 1. At a still pond (or other still body of water) look into the shallow depths of the pond at objects on the bottom (stones). Visually estimate how long a reach is necessary to pick up the stone, and compare that estimate of depth to the length the student has to immerse her arm in order to lift the stone out of the water. Observe objects (tree branches, plants) that are both in the water and in the air above. Dip a straight stick (branch, meter stick, canoe paddle) into the water.

Part 2. Fill a ten-gallon (minimum, larger is better) aquarium with water. Place a coin at the bottom of the tank. Visually estimate how long a reach is needed to remove the coin from the tank and compare that with the depth actually experienced. Insert a straight piece of glass tubing at an angle through the surface of the water.

DAY 2
Review Demonstration 8V1

When viewed from the air above, objects immersed in water were visually closer than they were according to reach. The objects appeared to be lifted toward the observer. This phenomenon is *refraction*. (When viewed from within the water, as occurs when swimming underwater, this phenomenon does not occur. The air-water interface is necessary. Viewed from underwater, objects in the air above look farther away. Students can sit underwater in a pool and observe this.) A consequence of this phenomenon is that objects are visually bent (while feeling straight to the touch) when immersed in water from the air above.

Demonstration 8V2a. Index of Refraction:

Place a quarter at the bottom and near the edge of a fish tank. Have each student look *straight* down onto the quarter through the water surface above. Hold a second quarter at the outside edge of the tank, parallel and next to the observed position of the quarter in the tank. Raise and lower the quarter on the outside of the tank until it appears adjacent to the quarter inside the tank, when viewed by the student looking through the water surface from above. A second student can measure the distance of the quarter outside the tank from the surface of the water. Record the depth of the outside quarter at the spot in which each student sees it as adjacent to the inside quarter. Measure the depth of water in the tank.

Demonstration 8V2b. Boundary Colors:

Place a piece of ceramic tile with a black pattern on a white background into a fish tank. *Carefully* observe the white-black boundaries of the pattern by looking at an angle through the top surface of the tank. *This effect is very subtle but very worthwhile!* [*Teacher's note: Extremely fine bands of color appear at the boundaries of the black-white pattern. Different color bands appear depending upon whether the boundary is viewed with white above black or black above white.*]

DAY 3
Review Demonstration 8V2

Each student should divide the depth of water in the tank (which is the depth of the quarter in the water) by the distance he perceived the quarter to be below the surface. The latter depth is the distance of the quarter outside of the tank from the water's surface. This ratio is the *index of refraction.* The accepted value of the index of refraction for an air-water interface is 1.33. The higher the index of refraction, the greater the visual lifting along the line of observation. The class can average all of the measurements and compare the resultant value with the accepted one. Typically, indices of refraction of glass are about 1.5, stronger than that of water. Plastics are higher. Diamond is 2.4. Students can observe a printed page through a thick plate of glass.

When viewed at an angle, the warm spectrum (red-orange-yellow) appears at the boundaries where the white of the tile is above the black, and the cool spectrum (violet-blue-cyan) appears at boundaries where the black is above the white.

Demonstration 8V3. Reflection, Refraction and Boundary Colors of Water Prisms:

Part 1. Ask students to look at images in the room through two adjacent vertical sides (i.e., a corner) of a water-filled aquarium and note their observations. They should compare these observations to what they see when looking directly at the scene, not through the glass and water.

Part 2. Ask students to look through a large water prism at images of the room. (*Caution: Do not look directly at the sun through the prism!*) Again, they should note their observations, paying particular attention to differences between looking through the prism and looking directly at the images. Each student can then be given a glass prism with which to make observations. To keep track of these observations, it is useful to note the position of the edge formed between the two sides of the prism through which the students are making their observations. (This edge and the third side, through which the students are not viewing, are parallel.) For example, is that edge up or down when the prism is held horizontally, or right or left when held vertically?

DAY 4
Review Demonstration 8V3

Depending upon the conditions of viewing, mirroring, refraction and color effects could be observed. It is our intention here to focus only on the refraction and color effect and not on mirroring. Compared to direct vision the images of the room appeared to be shifted to the edge of the aquarium formed by the two side surfaces through which the student was observing. (This is refraction due to looking through the air-glass-water-glass-air corner.) The same effect—that of images shifting toward the edge formed by the two surfaces through which viewing takes place— was seen with both the water and the glass prisms. The geometry of the aquarium near any of its edges is that of a prism.

The color bands noted in Demonstration 8V3, Part 2, occurred in the prism observations at viewed dark-light boundaries that were parallel to the axis of the prism. (The prism axis, prism viewing surfaces, and prism edges are parallel to each other and are perpendicular to the two ends.) The warm colors appeared when the viewed lighter color at the boundary was closer to the edge formed by the two viewing surfaces, and the cool colors appeared when the dark side of the boundary was closer to that edge.

Demonstration 8V4. Imaging with Lenses:

With the class standing at the other end of the room, hold a large (4"-dia. minimum) magnifying (double convex) glass in front of your face. The lens should be supported in a lens clamp. Starting with the lens close to your face, slowly move the lens away toward the students. Observe what happens to the image. In particular, note the distance from the face to the lens when the image is no longer recognizable as a facial feature. Clamp the handle of the lens clamp on a clamp stand. Starting next to and behind the lens, slowly move a sheet of printed material away from the lens. Repeat previous observations.

DAY 5
Review Demonstration 8V4
When viewed from afar, images seen through a magnifying glass appeared increasingly larger in size as the distance between the viewed object and the lens was increased. At a certain point, however, the image appeared chaotic and became unrecognizable. Further increasing the distance between the viewed object and the lens resulted in an inverted image whose size decreased from the originally very large (but then inverted) image. The distance at which the image "explodes" is called the *focal length.*

Demonstration 8V5. Determination of Focal Length and Magnification of Convex-Convex Lenses:

Pairs of students should draw a small (1/2") simple symbol, such as a letter, that looks different when turned upside down. Pass out a small convex-convex lens to each pair of students. Determine the focal length of their lens and the magnification at three-quarters, one-half, one-quarter and one and one-half times the focal length. Magnification is the ratio of the size of the image seen through the lens to the size of the image seen when viewed directly without a lens. Measurement can be done by placing the ruler directly on the lens while someone is observing. (Note: The student should observe from a distance of at least ten times that of the focal length of the lens.) Students can draw the images at each of the distances.

HYDRAULICS AND AERO-MECHANICS

DAY 1
Demonstration 8HA1. Pressure in Liquids:

Part 1. Completely fill a large and a small syringe with water. The syringes, obtainable from a laboratory supply house or a physician, must have the same size orifice (opening) where the needle is usually attached. It is unnecessary for the syringes to be fitted with needles for this demonstration. Holding them horizontally forcefully squirt the water from each syringe.

Part 2. Attach a 1ft length of plastic tubing to the larger of the syringes. Inserting the end of the tube into a reservoir of water, fill the barrel of the syringe half full. Fill the barrel of the smaller syringe half full with water and attach the syringe to the tube so that the tubing connects the two half-full syringes. When you give a signal, have two students press as forcefully as they can on each of the syringes in a kind of hydraulic push-of-war. (Be sure that the tubing is well connected so that the water does not leak in response to the pressure.)

Part 3. Using a small size bit, drill a hole in the *side* of the syringe near the orifice. Cover the orifice and squirt water through the drilled opening.

Part 4. Drill three equal-size holes on the sides of a one-liter plastic beverage bottle. One hole should be drilled near the top, another at the middle, and the last near the bottom. Completely fill the bottle with water and hold over a basin that is large enough to catch the water coming from the drilled holes.

DAY 2
Review of Demonstration 8HA1

Part 1. The smaller syringe squirted a greater distance than did the larger one. Because the smaller syringe has a smaller-diameter plunger, the same force (applied by the thumb) is exerted over a smaller area. This means that the force per unit area of surface on which it is applied is larger for the smaller syringe than for the larger one. The ratio of the force applied to a surface to the area of the surface is the *pressure*. Pressure is an indication of the intensity of an applied force. The import of pressure can be understood in relation to a thumbtack. The force at the head and pin end of the tack is the same while the pressure at the pin end is much greater than that at the head.

Part 2. The principle here is the same. Whatever difference in the force exerted by the two students is overcome by the higher pressure that is possible with the smaller syringe. The person holding that syringe consistently overwhelmed the person holding the larger one. This is the principle upon which a hydraulic lift, such as those found in an auto repair garage, is based. A pump pressurizes fluid in a small cylinder and piston. The pressure on the other side of the piston is communicated to a large piston cylinder combination, which lifts the car. Since the pressure in the second cylinder acts over a large area the force exerted is much larger than in the smaller cylinder. On the other hand, a large movement of the smaller piston produces only a small movement of the larger piston, and therefore only a small amount of lift. This can be easily demonstrated with a portable hydraulic two-ton jack. (This is the type that rolls on metal wheels and is pumped by a handle. It is widely available in auto supply departments or stores.)

Part 3. The third part of the demonstration showed that the direction of the squirting is independent of the direction of plunger motion. It indicates that pressure acts in all directions and not only in the direction of the force applied.

Part 4. In the final part of the demonstration, we saw that the farther the hole was from the water surface the greater the distance that the water is squirted. Here the pressure is due to the weight of the height of water above the hole rather than to someone's pushing. (The atmospheric pressure also contributes to the pressure of the water by pushing on each area of the water surface with the atmosphere. However, since the contribution of atmospheric pressure is the same for all three holes, the greater pressure at the bottom hole is due to the greater weight of the water above it.)

Demonstration 8HA2. Pressure depends upon Height of Liquid Column:

Part 1. Fill a set of Pascal's communicating tubes [see ASLS] with water. Note the height of water in the tubes. Pour some water into one of the tubes and observe the resulting heights.

Part 2. Fill an aquarium to within two inches of the top. Place a 1½" ball of clay into the tank. (The clay sinks to the bottom.) Give a similar-sized piece to each student. Instruct each student to form it in such a way that it floats in the water. As the students finish their "boats" they can test the design in the aquarium. The students can retrieve unsuccessful models from the bottom and try again.

Part 3. Weigh an empty 100ml graduated cylinder using a beam balance. Fill the cylinder with 70 ml of water and reweigh. Place a wooden pencil on the balance along with the cylinder of water and weigh again. Now, place the pencil into the cylinder of water on the beam balance. Note that the total weight does not change and that the water level in the cylinder increases. Record the volume level of the water in the cylinder with the pencil floating in it. Repeat with a common #6 nail.

DAY 3
Review Demonstration 8HA2
Part 1. The height and not the volume of Pascal's communicating tubes determined pressure. If the volume were the determining factor, then the pressure due to the water in the tubes of larger volume would push the water in the lower volume tubes to higher levels.

Part 2. What was common about the boats that successfully floated? Relative to the amount of clay used, a large interior volume was required. This was achieved by those who made the shape with thin walls.

Part 3. Using the data obtained in the demonstration find the density of water. Density is the ratio of the mass of an object to its volume. (At sea level on earth, a gram mass is equal to one gram weight. In effect, then, the density is the ratio of weight to volume.) Subtract the weight of the empty cylinder from that of the cylinder filled. (The 70 mls of water should weigh 70 gms. Thus, the density of water is 1 gm per milliliter.) The increase in volume found when the pencil displaced water was numerically equal to the weight of the displaced water. For an object to float, the pressure of the water pushing up on the floating body must equal the pressure pushing down due to the weight of the object. As the body is placed in the water, it sinks. The water pressure on the object increases due to the increasing height of water above the floating object. The object sinks until there is sufficient height of water to produce sufficient pressure to balance that of the weight of the object. If the water pressure is still less than that due to the weight of the object when the top of the object is at the water's surface, then the object sinks. Our measurements with the floating pencil show that the condition of equal water pressure and pressure due to the weight of the object occurs when *the weight of the water displaced by the object is equal to the weight of the object*. This is *Archimedes Principle (Eureka!)*. (The story is well known of Archimedes' recognition of this principle while taking a bath and then running down the street shouting, "Eureka, I have it.") In the case of the nail, its weight was more than that of the water that it displaced.

Demonstration 8HA3. Air Pressure:

When the students have seen the effect that pressure has on the relationship between solid objects and a liquid, they can then begin to appreciate the relationship between solid objects and a "finer" fluid: air.

Part 1. Cover the opening of a syringe with your thumb. Pull the plunger out and watch it return when you let go of it.

Part 2. Fit a one-hole stopper with a six-inch glass tube. Stopper a large flask filled with water and invert it. Repeat with a two-hole stopper fitted with a single glass tube in one of the holes.

DAY 4
Review Demonstration 8HA3

Part 1. The air pressure in the syringe decreased as the volume of the syringe was increased (by pulling out the plunger). Since the atmospheric pressure (that acts on the piston handle) was greater than the pressure of the air in the cylinder of the syringe, the piston was pushed back in when it was let go. The piston stopped when the cylinder volume decreased sufficiently that the air pressure in the syringe again equaled and balanced the atmospheric pressure.

Part 2. The water was prevented from pouring out of the flask by the pressure (atmospheric) of the outside air. With a two-hole stopper, air could enter through one opening while water poured out of the other.

Air and water are both fluids. Just as water pressure at a particular position depends on the height (and weight) of the column of water above that position, so does air pressure depend on the height (and weight) of the column of air above the position where the pressure is measured. Atmospheric air pressure decreases with increased height. While ascending high mountains, the atmospheric air pressure decreases. Since the air pressure within the inner ear becomes increasingly larger than that of the atmosphere the inner ear is caused to bulge out. Swallowing clears the Eustachian tube and balances the inner and outer air pressures. The opposite occurs while descending.

Demonstration 8HA4. Magdeburg Hemispheres:

A demonstration of Magdeburg hemispheres [see ASLS] is a wonderful way to finish this subject. They can be evacuated with a simple plastic hand-held and -operated vacuum pump. The hemispheres not only demonstrate the astounding force of atmospheric pressure acting on a surface but also have fascinating

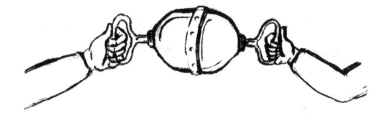

historical significance. Many illustrations show crowds gaping at fair grounds as two horses are unable to pull the spheres apart. Robert Boyle is reputed to have been inspired to do his research on pressurizing gases (leading to Boyle's Law) after seeing von Guericke demonstrating his hemispheres as a young man.

It is a simple matter to calculate the force that holds the Magdeburg hemispheres together. Von Guericke's original spheres were two ft (24 in) in diameter. The surface area of one of von Guericke's spheres was $\pi(D/2)^2 = \pi(24/6)^2 = 452$ in^2. Multiplying the surface area by atmospheric pressure (14.7 lbs/in^2) yields the force holding the hemispheres together, 6644lbs! No wonder horses could not pull them apart. A similar calculation for typical four-inch-diameter demonstration spheres gives a force of 185 pounds.

ELECTROMAGNETISM

In the eighth grade the electrical and magnetic phenomena coalesce into a single experience. In the first demonstration, a version of Oersted's famous experiment, an electrical condition and a magnetic field occur simultaneously. This occurrence is the basis for an electric motor. By the end of the study of electromagnetism each student should be able to clearly describe how each component of an electric motor works and how it could be changed to make the motor spin more quickly.

Electric motors are found everywhere, yet few people understand the principles on which they operate. When they finally grasp how a motor works the students feel empowered.

DAY 1
Demonstration 8EM1. Oersted's Experiment:

CAUTION! AUTOMOBILE BATTERIES CAN BE VERY DANGER-OUS. FOLLOW DIRECTIONS EXACTLY AS DESCRIBED. This demonstration should be done with students wearing safety glasses. Students should NOT touch any wires. Do NOT connect a wire across the terminals. (The result of doing so was demonstrated last year.) Do NOT touch both terminals at the same time. Do NOT touch grounded metal objects while touching one of the terminals. Do NOT do electrical demonstrations in the presence of water.

These warnings are presented to impress upon the teacher the necessity for working in a safe and proper manner. The experiences are profound for the students and are well worth doing.

Either obtain a twelve-volt automobile headlight bulb from an automotive supply store or remove a headlight assembly (socket and bulb) from an automobile. (The advantage of the headlight assembly is that its terminals provide simple connection of electrical leads. Leads to the bulb will need to be soldered. Alternatively, an automobile headlight light socket and bulb can be purchased from an auto parts department.)

Wrap solid copper wire around the positive (anode) terminal of a fully charged automobile battery, leaving a straight one-inch extension above. Do the same for the negative (cathode) terminal. Attach three foot-long leads to both sides of the twelve-volt light bulb or light bulb assembly. Using an alligator clip, attach one of these leads to the cathode terminal of the battery. Similarly, attach the other lead to the anode terminal. Stretching one of the leads taut between two ring stands, bring as large a compass as

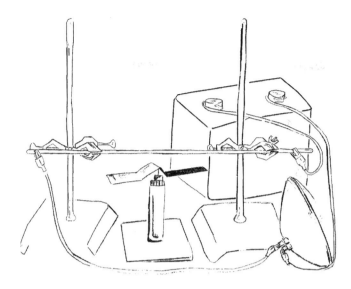

possible just above the wire. (We recommend a demonstration compass.) Now place the compass just beneath the wire.

DAY 2
Review Demonstration 8EM1

This is a version of Oersted's famous experiment. From previous experience we know that a battery is a condition for electricity and a compass is a condition for magnetism. In this case, the compass moved in the vicinity of a metal wire that connected two battery terminals that were in an electrical condition. Since the compass reacted, the space around the wire into which the compass was inserted was magnetic. The structure of this magnetism was revealed by the reaction of the compass. That the compass lined up in a plane perpendicular to the wire and pointed in opposite directions when above and below the wire led us to infer that the structure of the magnetism was circular about the wire. This intuition is the source of inspiration for the following experience.

Demonstration 8EM2. The Form of the Magnetic Field That Is Associated with a Wire That Is Electrified:

Part 1. Use the same apparatus as in Demonstration 8EM1, this time supporting the wire vertically and passing it through a stiff horizontal piece of paper. Sprinkle iron filings evenly onto the paper. Remove the iron filings and repeat the demonstration with a number of small inexpensive compasses of the type available in souvenir shops, bubble gum dispensers and laboratory supply houses.

Part 2. Using four feet of 22-gauge (.025"-diameter) copper lacquered or enameled magnet wire, wind eight turns of wire around a baby food jar and then remove the jar. Using a penknife, scrape the lacquer or enamel insulation from one inch of either end to expose the copper. Attach one end of the coiled wire to a terminal of a six-volt lantern battery. Support the coil of wire so that its plane is vertical and lies in the N-S direction. Slide the coil over a compass, which is held in the usual (horizontal) position. Briefly touch the other end of the wire to the other terminal of

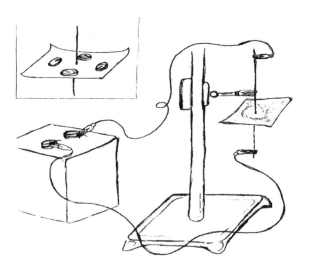

the battery, and then remove. Rotate the position of the coil about a vertical axis and repeat for several different positions. (Find and note the position where there is no change in the compass reading.)

Part 3. Using a commercial laboratory demonstration coil (a Gilley coil from a student demonstration kit) connected to the six-volt lantern battery, bring a common #6 iron nail (used for nailing 2 x 4s together) to the opening of the coil. Note the effect. Then, while it is energized, move the coil so that the nail rotates into a vertical position from its originally horizontal position. With the nail in place, try to pick up some paper clips. Try the same without the nail in the coil. Replace the nail inside the coil and then disconnect one of the terminals.

DAY 3
Review of Demonstration 8EM2
Part 1. When connected to the battery and light bulb the iron filings on the paper moved and formed a pattern of approximately concentric circular rings; they did not line up perpendicular to the wire. The small compasses did the same as the iron filings.

Part 2. The compass aligned itself perpendicularly to the plane of the coil.

Part 3. The nail aligned itself as did the compass needle and positioned itself symmetrically in the coil (i.e., it centered itself with regard to both the axis of the coil and its length). Here, the many more windings in the coil compared to the eight-turn loop produced a much stronger effect. (In general, more windings produce a stronger effect.) Also, with the nail in place, the magnet was much stronger than when the nail was not present. These phenomena reveal that the space around a wire that is in a circuit with an electrified body is different from ordinary space: Iron materials move in space without any material body pushing or pulling them. Such a space is called a *magnetic field*. The phenomenon in which a magnetic field appears in the presence of an electric circuit is called *electromagnetism*.

Demonstration 8EM3. Electromagnets and Electric Bells:

Part 1. Connect two Gilley coils around a U-shaped iron or steel core as shown in the diagram. Pick up a nail, steel paper clips, or a steel bar. For an even stronger effect dissectible electromagnets are available from laboratory suppliers.

Part 2. Demonstrate an electric bell. (It is advisable to wire a bell kit together on a wooden base so that the students can easily see the circuit connections without a tangle of wires.)

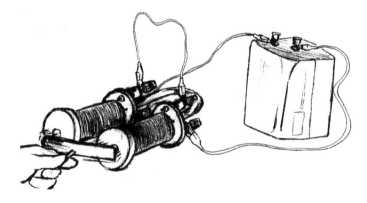

Day 4
Review of Demonstration 8EM3

Part 1. Note that the configuration in which the ends of a U-shaped iron or steel bar were inserted into two electrified coils produced a very strong effect.

Part 2. Describe how the bell worked: When the coil was electrified by closing the switch it became an electromagnet that attracted the clapper. As the clapper moved to the electromagnet it hit the bell and the electrical contacts were pulled apart so that the circuit was broken. When the circuit was broken, the coil is no longer electrified and was therefore no longer a magnet. Therefore the clapper was no longer attracted and returned to its normal position. But in its normal position electrical contact was reestablished and the cycle repeated itself as long as the switch was closed. Students should draw a diagram of this in the open and closed position.

Demonstration 8EM4. The DC Motor:

Part 1. Set up apparatus as in Demonstration 8EM1 without connecting wires to battery terminals. Holding an end of the wire in each hand begin to alternately make contact by reversing the leads between the terminals. That is, the lead held in the right hand will be contacted, released and switched between the terminals and the same for the lead held in the left hand. When the right hand is making contact with the positive terminal, the left hand lead is at the same time being contacted with the negative terminal. As this is done the compass needle will swing back and forth. With the proper rhythmical switching the compass needle will begin to spin in a circle. It is this rhythm (and spinning) that the teacher should attain.

Part 2. Assemble and wire a DC demonstration electric motor of the type that employs permanent magnets (St. Louis motor). Connect terminals to a 6V battery and observe. Rotate the brush assembly on the commutater to demonstrate the change in motor speed with position of the brushes relative to the commutater.

DAY 5
Review Demonstration 8EM4

What was required for the compass needle to spin in a circle? (Answer: A rhythmic reversal of electrical condition at the wire leads. Since a reversal of the electrical condition resulted in motion of the compass needle and motion of the needle is what reveals the magnetic field, we can conclude that reversing the electric connections produced a change in the magnetic field. The back-and-forth oscillation means that the field itself was being reversed. The circular motion was produced when the field reversal was timed so that the motion of the needle "carries through" the interval during switching, toward the other side so that when the new field is established the compass keeps going around [instead of falling back].)

"What caused the switching on the motor? (Answer: The electrical contacts are on the shaft of the motor itself. Brushing the electrical leads from the battery terminal made an electrical connection with the rotating contacts of the motor. The contacts from the battery leads are called *brushes*. Notice that there are two positions on the motor shaft where there is no contact material. The brushes at these positions are equivalent to the interval between hand switching. The assembly on the motor shaft, including the brushes and rotating contacts is called a *commutater*. When the brushes changed from one rotating contact to the other, the electrical condition at the rotating contacts had been switched. Here the switching occurred not at the battery but at the motor shaft.

The students need to look at the motor, rotate it by hand, and *see* this for themselves. We have already seen that such switching means that the magnetic field too is switched. The rotating coil (called an *armature*) with its magnetic field moved in the magnetic field of the permanent magnets in an analogous way to the compass moving in the magnetic field of the coil in Part 1 of Demonstration 8EM4. In the compass, the permanent magnet spins in the magnetic field of the coil, while in the motor the magnetic field of a coil spins in the field of a permanent magnet.)

Demonstration 8EM5. A Student Built Motor:

An excellent way to complete the elementary school physics education is for the students (individually or in groups) to build their own electric motors. A very good motor kit for this purpose is available from the Waldorf Publications (WP). (See Apparatus and Supplies List and Sources for details.) This kit consists of simple materials such as wire, nails and a wood base. Using common tools, such as a Phillips screwdriver, needle nose pliers, sandpaper, a soldering iron and wire cutters, the students make the motor themselves. (Only the commutater contacts (brushes) are pre-formed.) This motor employs an electromagnet rather than a permanent magnet to produce the field. Plan to spend several afternoon periods for completion of the motor.

Apparatus and Supplies
List and Sources

The supplies and sources listed in this section are grouped according to grade level and, within that level, according to subject. In some cases the same apparatuses are used in different grades. To enable the teacher of a particular grade to gather what is needed without having to refer to a previous grade, the required supplies and apparatus are repeated. Kits for each grade are available from Waldorf Publications. Several alternate sources of apparatus are also listed.

The source key is:

WP	Waldorf Publications
HW	Hardware Store
APS	Auto Parts and Supplies Store
SS	Scientific Supply Company Catalog

ADDRESSES

Waldorf Publications
38 Main Street
Chatham, NY 12037
Tel: (518) 634-2222
email: robin@waldorf-research.org
To order Science Kits: www.waldorfpublications.org

Frey Scientific, Beckley Cardy Group
100 Paragon Parkway, Mansfield, OH 44903
Tel (888) 222-1332

Central Scientific Company (CENCO)
3300 Cenco Parkway, Franklin Park, IL 60131
Tel: (800) 262-3262

Cole-Parmer Instrument Company
625 East Bunker Court, Vernon Hills, IL 60061
Tel: (800) 323-4340

Fisher Scientific (Fisher Science Education)
4855 Frontage Road, Burr Ridge, IL 60521
Tel: (800) 955-1177

Sargent-Welch Scientific
P.O. Box 5229, Buffalo Grove, IL 60089
Tel: (800) 727-4368

SIXTH GRADE

Sound-Acoustics
½" copper pipe of various lengths (HW)
String
Monochord (WP Kit)
Fine grain sand (WP Kit)
Lycopodium powder (WP Kit)
Chladni plate (WP Kit)

Visual Experience – Optics
Electric light dimmer (HW)
Lamp and bulb, 300–500 watt minimum
Metal food can
Black spray paint (HW)
Paper and paint

Warmth and Cold

Bunsen burner or propane torch (SS or HW)
Cast iron plumber's spoon (HW)
Lead-free tin solder (HW)
Basin
Candle
Thin steel wire (HW)
Two 10-pound weights
Three 1000ml beakers (SS)
Clamp stand with ring clamp (SS)
Ink
Safety goggles for entire class (SS)
Hot mitts (heat resistant gloves) (SS)
Ceramic fiber wire gauze pad (SS)

Electricity and Magnetism

Rabbit fur (WP Kit)
Pith ball (WP Kit)
Glass rod (WP Kit)
Silk cloth (WP Kit)
Amber necklace
Contact paper
Cotton balls
Electroscope (WP Kit)
Magnetite (lodestone) (WP Kit)
Demonstration compass (WP Kit)
½" diameter x 3ft steel reinforcing rod (HW)
Small sledgehammer (HW)
Clay and board
1/8" diameter x 18" steel rod (HW)
Clamp stand and clamps

SEVENTH GRADE

Warmth – Cold
1000ml beaker (SS)
Large metal and wooden spoons
Safety goggles for entire class (SS)
Clamp stand (SS)
Ceramic fiber wire gauze pad (SS)
Four empty metal cans
Gravel
Sand
Sheared wool
Bunsen burner or propane torch (SS or HW)
Clamps for clamp stand (SS)
Vernier calipers (accurate to .001 inch) (SS or HW)
Ball and ring apparatus (WP Kit)
250ml flask (SS)
Rubber stopper assortment (SS)
Glass tubing (SS)
Thin-wall metal can (maple syrup can)

Visual Experience – Optics
Rough and smooth metal pieces
Rough and smooth wood pieces
Large mirror (2 feet x 4 feet if possible)
String
4" x 6" mirrors (for student groups of 2)
Candle
Material for darkening room (opaque paper & tape)

Electrical Phenomena
1" x 5" copper strip for each student (WP Kit)
1" x 5" zinc strip for each student (WP Kit)

Various wire leads (2–4ft) with insulated
alligator clips at ends (WP Kit)
Six 400ml beakers (SS)
Pure salt (kosher)
Filter paper (WP Kit)
12-volt automobile battery (APS)
Jumper cables (APS)
22-gauge copper wire (WP Kit)

Mechanics
8ft x 4" x 4" wood post (without knots)
Sturdy saw horse (HW)
Assortment of weights (2.5–35 pounds)
Steel cable (HW)
Crow bar (HW)
4–6ft steel bar or pipe (HW)
1/4"-drive socket wrench with 1/4" to 3/8"
adapter (for automobile wheel lug nut socket)
(APS or HW)
3/8"-drive socket wrench (APS or HW)
1/2"- drive socket wrench (APS or HW)
3/8"-drive socket for lug nut (APS or HW)
1/2"-drive socket for lug nut (APS or HW)
1/2"-drive breaker bar or 4–6 ft x 1" diameter
hollow steel pipe (APS or HW)
1/2" to 3/8" adapter (APS or HW)
3/8" x 6" extension (APS or HW)

EIGHTH GRADE

Warmth – Thermal Physics
Pinwheel
Incense sticks (punk sticks)
Mason jars

Visual Phenomena – Refraction
Ten-gallon (minimum) aquarium
Meter stick (SS)
Ceramic tile with black and white pattern
Two large water prisms (WP Kit)
Glass prisms for each student (WP Kit)
4" double convex glass lens (WP Kit)
1½" diameter double convex lenses for each student
(WP Kit)

Hydraulics and Aero-Mechanics
Various syringes (WP Kit)
Rubber tubing to fit syringe ends (WP Kit)
1-liter plastic water bottle
Portable two-ton hydraulic jack (APS)
Pascal's communicating tubes (WP Kit)
Clay
Balance scale (SS)
100ml graduated cylinder (SS)
Two-hole rubber stopper (SS)
Glass tubing (to fit rubber stopper) (SS)
100ml flask (SS)
Magdeburg hemispheres (WP Kit)

Electromagnetism

12-volt automobile battery (APS)
Automobile headlight and assembly (APS)
Assortment of electrical leads w/alligator clips (WP Kit)
Electric leads with alligator clips (WP Kit)
16-gauge copper wire (WP Kit)
Two clamp stands
Demonstration compass (WP Kit)
Iron filings (WP Kit)
Four small (inexpensive) compasses (WP Kit)
22-gauge lacquered copper wire (WP Kit)
2 demonstration coils (Gilley coils) (WP Kit)
Six-volt lantern batter (SS or HW)
Common #6 nail (HW)
Electric bell kit (WP Kit)
DC demonstration St. Louis motor (WP Kit)
Electric motor kit for each students or pair of students
        (WPKit)

References

1. Herman von Baravalle, *Waldorf Education for America*, Parker Courtney, Chestnut Ridge, NY, 1998, pp. 137–139.
2. Manfred von Mackensen, *A Phenomena-Based Physics, Vol. 1 Grade 6*, AWSNA Publications, Fair Oaks, CA, 1994.
3. Stephen Edelglass, Georg Maier, Hans Gebert, and John Davy, *The Marriage of Sense and Thought; Imaginative Participation in Science*, Lindisfarne, Hudson, NY, 1997.

86938281R00061

Made in the USA
Columbia, SC
16 January 2018